You Can't So You Don't

T. Raheyyu Hope

Dedication

This book is dedicated to those who feel lost, underappreciated, and hopeless. I dedicate this book to you because you are more valuable than you think you are. Allow yourself to soar above the muck and mire of life to heights you never imagined.

I pray your tomorrows are better than your todays and your todays are better than your yesterdays.

Acknowledgment

A special thanks to those who helped put this book together. Thank you for your hard work and dedication.

A special acknowledgment to my dad, Wesley Ramsey, who has been a pivotal part of my life. I will always love you and miss you deeply. Thank you, mom, for allowing me to use your poem to edify those who need encouragement and enlightenment.

Finally, a special thanks to those who purchased this book and found the contents to be a healing balm to their heart, mind, and soul.

About the Author

Raheyyu Hope, AKA Blessed Hope, has two children, a daughter who is a Graphics Artist in N.Y., and a son with special needs. She believes God will heal her son one day from his disorder.

Raheyyu has struggled in the past with anxiety and depression for most of her life. She was able to overcome through the power of prayer and the support of those around her. There are times when she feels the anxiety and depression trying to creep back into her life, but she doesn't allow it to overtake or overwhelm her.

Raheyyu is also an aspiring singer/songwriter and has been singing since the tender age of 10 at a Baptist church in Newark, N.J. She transitioned to worshiping at a non-denominational church in Paterson, N.J.

Unfortunately, Raheyyu Hope had dark days during which she left her first love and stopped singing for many years. However, she found her lost-passion for singing again after the untimely and tragic death of her father. She is now pursuing music once again, allowing her heart to heal. She hopes to do the same for others. She also hopes to inspire those dealing with anxiety, depression, doubt, and fear with this book. She wants you to know that you are not alone in your journey. This book seeks to encourage anyone who needs a jumpstart in their pursuits.

Raheyyu Hope has an AA degree in Business, a BA degree in Psychology, and is pursuing a Master's degree in Counseling which she will attain in 2021.

Preface

I feel like so many chapters in my life have taken a turn to this new journey of self-discovery. So, I decided to go on this journey a few years ago. Although it has taken a few years to get to my desired goal, I am glad I have finally begun. Unfortunately, the pandemic hit and delayed a lot of things, but I am still moving forward. Who would have ever thought that life would take such an unpredictable turn in 2020? I had so many plans and dreams at the beginning of the year, and now everything is on hold. Well, I guess not everything. Instead of focusing on releasing my music, I'm releasing my book first.

The world is ever-changing, and I don't necessarily feel the need to change with it, but change I will. I still hold the same values and beliefs in God and know that he is the Lord over my life. I still like the same music and the same foods, friends, relatives, family, and so on so forth. However, there is a need to evolve and reinvent **me**. The same old me just ain't working anymore, and it's getting old.

Sometimes reinventing yourself has a risk, but there is also a reward waiting along the way and at the end if you succeed. The risk is stepping out of your comfort zone and allowing yourself to be vulnerable before others. To accept the criticisms as well as compliments along the journey of discovery. It seems quite strange to still have the desire to pursue this idea with the pandemic and all, but pursue it, I will. Paul Tillich once said, *"Decision is a risk rooted in the courage of being free."* If we allow fear to stop us from doing what we truly desire to do, then we will never complete it.

What is it you really want from life? Can you really make the change happen, or are you too scared to go after what you want? If you have ever felt the need to evolve and reinvent, I hope you will pursue that journey, and maybe this book can help motivate you.

We live in a world where people are constantly seeking to make a difference. They are tired of the rhetoric, and no change has occurred. When will things get done? When will we see real change in our world for the better and stop talking about it and start making a noticeable difference?

I have decided to start making the change within myself, and hopefully, it will reverberate, and others will do the same whether that positive change comes through writing a book, singing a song, painting a picture, or producing a poem. It could also come through advocating for those who don't have a voice, but it can't happen until you decide to make it happen.

What change will you make, or have you already made one?

Foreword

Having experienced the 'You 'Can't' movement of life, I chose to write this book from a personal perspective of what I have experienced throughout my life. I hope that this book will help someone move forward and accomplish their dreams despite being told the infamous two-word phrase, 'You Can't.'

This book is not for those who have arrived, who have made it, or have exceeded their expectations. Rather, this book is for those who were told they can't, so they don't aspire to move forward. Some feel like they are at an impasse in their life. You feel invisible, unheard, and silenced by your doubts and/or because of negative feedback from someone in your life.

I didn't write this book from a Christian perspective. I am not a Pastor or Theologian who teaches the scriptures. Furthermore, I do not speak for all Christians even though I share a common belief with my fellow devotees in believing in the following Biblical verse:

"For God so loved the World, that he gave his only begotten Son, that whosoever believeth in him should not perish, but have everlasting life." John 3:16.

Contents

Chapter 1: You Can't

How many times have you been told that you aren't smart enough, pretty enough, or just don't fit in? Or you can't do a certain thing, go to a certain place, or achieve a certain level of success! Perhaps you have tried to ignore such people, but over time, it overwhelmed you. I have realized that failing at something is the single best motivator.

There are people who will always remind you that you are a failure or not accomplished. There will be times when their reminders are the last thing you need. You do not need a refresher about your failures in your already deplorable state. As you go on in life, you will make bad decisions, and that's normal. It's the name of the game, but you might begin to forget all your successes.

You would soon doubt everything you've done all your life only because you listened to someone's discourse for so long that you begin to believe it. The lies and ploys of your enemies worked. You lowered your gate and let them shoot arrows right through you. It's time you stop the fiery darts heading toward you. It's time you bring a self-revolution.

The first thing to brand at the back of your mind is the fact that you're treasured. Your abilities are valuable to yourself and the people around you. You can make an impact, regardless of what you have been told. You could land a huge fish in any organization you start at. Every single person on this planet has the potential to make it big and change the world. It's just about believing in yourself. Don't think it's only you who's going through this phase; many do! I used to listen to the negative words from people who didn't have my best interest. Sometimes, it's not so blatantly in your face but said to you in subtler ways. I used to get greatly affected by what people thought of me. I couldn't stand the insults hurled at me; they really hurt me. Once they see the impact they have on you, your mental state, life, and actions, these people love it even more. It's like a twisted fantasy of manipulation.

Instead of lashing back at these people, you should push them away. If you've submitted yourself to them for a long time, chances are, they know all your weak points and could easily destroy your newly found strength. First of all, you must reveal who these people are. They can be people in your family, workplace, people you might interact with outside your home, or even your friends. I hate saying it, but yes, some of your friends might be maintaining a dual identity. They might appear sweet, but they could have stabbed you multiple times behind your back. They do not offer you anything but distraction and hopelessness! I do want to mention that you shouldn't start doubting all your friends now. Over time, you must have developed a good judgment. You'll know who'll yank you up as you hang from the brink of a precipitous cliff and who'll step on your fingers, so you fall to your death. Just keep in mind to never go mountain climbing with friends you don't know too well. Seems dramatic? Friendships are!

I feel like it's absolutely crucial to educate yourself about the two types of criticisms. Destructive criticism only focuses on the downsides of your hobbies, work, possessions, and appearance, snubbing completely all the effort, time, and resources put in. People who always resort to this sort of criticism are the ones you should stay away from. I will talk more about these people in more detail in a later chapter. Alternatively, constructive criticism involves highlighting what went wrong while also shifting the spotlight to some of the things that you wonderfully did. This kind of criticism can help you build upon your skills, talents, or whatever you endeavor to do. The people who have your best interest at heart will help you with positive critique to push you forward. They will invest in your future, offer sound advice, encourage you, and speak the truth to you with love.

There was a time I would just go through life believing the lies and misconceptions, but now, I can identify true character builders from random agitators. For example, some drivers on the road whiz past you, cut you off and sideswipe you. They blow their horn at you because you are actually driving within the speed limit. They're doing something wrong, so they want others to follow their path. This also rings true in success. The random agitators are mostly unsuccessful in their activities, and so they don't want you to go further than them. My character builder was, let's call her, the pushy supermarket lady. She decided to push my cart out of the way and then dared to barge her way through without saying excuse me or pardon me. And when I remarked, "don't push my cart," she started yelling and hurling all kinds of insults at me. The insult that got me the most was when she called me 'the typical black girl.'

What is the typical black girl, and what does she look like? We all know the children's rhyme, "sticks and stones will break my bones, but names will never hurt me." A well-known saying was created to come against bullying. Well, sticks and stones hurt, and so do words. Harsh words truly hurt whether we like to admit it or not. I am guilty of saying things I didn't mean to say and hurt people in ways that I did not intend. However, I have realized my mistake and apologized whenever I could. I've had to eat my words and take a look at myself and rethink my actions.

When the supermarket incident occurred, I couldn't control my emotions and reacted negatively. I shouldn't, but I did! I'm learning how to handle situations like those better now. Sometimes, it takes a lifetime to heal from hurtful words. Believe me; I have been called many names throughout my life. Thank God, I have overcome those names because there is a *"name that is above every name and that name is Jesus"* (Philippians 2:9).

People can only do things to us that we permit them to do. When people see that you won't allow them to do what they want to you, they will better understand how you want to be treated by others. I decided to work on my reaction to people like the "pushy supermarket lady" and found an alternative way to respond. I should have handled it better than I did, and for that, I am disappointed in myself, but she was wrong to say that. It was incredibly rude and uncivilized to call someone out like that and especially by linking me to a stereotype. I will never forget that interaction, partially because it scarred me for many years and partly because it made me more aware of the social world's negativities. There are green, calm areas in the world, but those are landlocked by wildfires and dark places. It's just the reality, although I wish with all my heart that it wasn't. Negativity is all around us. Even if I have progressively become less prone, there are many who are still in calamitous situations. Even though I recognize it's impossible for me to empower even a fraction of that population, I might be able to impact some people through this book. That is good enough for me!

The journey of constantly hearing "You Can't" makes me so mad at times because it is a self-destructive term. At the start, it might not appear to be a problem, but eventually, it can make you lose all hope in yourself and even God. Now, this is something you never want to do. The Lord is always there even when you're alone on a stormy night, stuck in a cave. Once you've lost hope, your whole perspective on life changes to a great extent - you could say hopelessness is like a pair of glasses with superglue on them. Once you put them on, you see the world through a negative lens. You would start to think of the worst possible outcome for everything, and that's incredibly unhealthy. It forces you to search and find a perfect world, which is undoubtedly a wild goose chase. There is nothing, and I mean nothing on this whole planet, free from flaws and disadvantages. This means you'll never find anything that you actually want to do, ultimately making you feel even worse. It's super dangerous at this point, resulting in severe stress, anxiety, and depression. I know people who have just given up on their dreams because they ate the "You Can't" delicacy.

I often wonder how much has been missed because someone didn't paint the picture or write a song that would have influenced the world. It kills me to think that so many people decided not to pursue whatever endeavor that could have potentially made a difference. When people pursue their dreams, they change their lives and, possibly, even the world. However, many stories never get to see their ends because they fell victim to the lies. I always remind myself that "I can do all things through Christ that strengthens me" Philippians 4:13. Being successful and accomplished is every individual's dream. Don't lose that desire and urge in you. It's happened at multiple points in my life. There were times when I thought I might not make it, but I did. I don't consider myself an accomplished person. However, I consider myself successful because I have decided not to give up and continue pursuing my goals. Since I was a little girl, I aspired to be so many things in life. However, I listened to others' negativity, who told me I couldn't do what I wanted. I grew up in a household that taught me to be the best I could be and never settle for less. Contrary to what I was taught, the counsel of negativity overrode the basic principle taught in my childhood. Such is the strength of society. It can turn you into something you never wanted to be. Sometimes that something can be a diabolical monstrosity of a person!

I want to share a story from my high school days. It was one of the most disappointing days of my entire life. I remember when a guidance counselor told me that college wasn't an option. I felt there were no other options for me. I had hit a dead end. My potential to achieve anything in life was null and void. I wasn't a bad student with D's or F's on my report card.

I just didn't fit in with a future college student's fixed model according to the required norm. I was supposed to heat myself up, pour myself into the preset mold, and hope to God that the consistency didn't mess up. I didn't do that. I couldn't make myself do that. College for me had a large spray-painted 'X' on it. I began thinking about my other options and even thought about enlisting in the Army or becoming a Corrections Officer.

As I pondered the decision, I found that neither seemed to be what I wanted to do. I accepted that moment that I wouldn't go to college at all, and instead, I would work as a secretary for a prestigious company. It wasn't an easy decision. I eventually tried to go back to college part-time, but my confidence was lagging, and I found myself on academic probation. I pretty much gave up, and it would take years to get back on track. The options for me seemed darkened by whispers that said: "you are not college material, just give up." However, I didn't remain stagnant, opened my eyes, set my hand to the plow, and didn't look back.

It took all my might, but I knew I was doing the right thing for myself. It is always good to have options, but mine were locked, so I decided that if no one else gave me options, I would create them. I would continue to evolve and recreate myself rather than become stagnant.

Always know that stationary water provides the perfect environmental conditions for some of the most dangerous diseases humankind has ever seen. Hence, remaining stagnant or stationery can be extremely detrimental to us humans as well.

Chapter 2: What Path Are You On?

Now that we've talked a little about the hurdles you'll most definitely face throughout life, let's move on to determining what path to take. The answer might seem simple at the start when I say it, but let that sink in; it has a difficult application.

The path of fulfillment and contentment is what I think everyone should take. Many people struggle with their depression and sadness even when it appears that they're on top of their game. They're mostly suffering because of a lack of fulfillment and contentment. Everyone wants to be fulfilled, but is everyone successful at it? No! A common desire among religious people is to live a life based on the salvation of Jesus Christ. It is important to note that there is no universal way to define fulfillment, as everyone might have their own definition of it. The book definition is *"the achievement of something desired."* The last word is what brings in adversity.

Desires vary on individual, historical, and cross-cultural levels. The usual self-fulfilling element in most people's lives is wealth and material possessions. However, money isn't everything. Some people might feel fulfilled after having the experience they might have wanted for a long time, such as bungee-jumping or skydiving.

The Power of Self-Actualization

Related to fulfillment is the concept of self-actualization. As the name suggests, it is the point at which one believes they've peaked in their existence. They have achieved what they always wanted. This is only temporary bliss, though, because the self-actualization point shifts to something else once you've reached your previous point. It's a never-ending process. You set a goal and devise a strategy to achieve it.

Once you've done what you dreamed of, would you just lay around twiddling your thumbs, waiting for life to pass you by? Of course not! You would now set another target to achieve. It's an unlimited cycle of achieving life goals then setting yet some more. This goes on till death does the individual and his/her objectives apart.

Self-fulfillment and actualization are a state of temporary accomplishment. That accomplishment remains in your mind as an imaginary medal or trophy. You are reminded by yourself or by others about it, and it makes you feel good about yourself, but there isn't much more to it.

"You made it somewhere, so what?" your mind will whisper. "You want more."

That's the problem. Now don't get me wrong, every person deserves to live sparkling lives and progress to the highest possible levels in life, but the greed to always have excessive amounts of anything is unhealthy. Our brains are wired in a way that we always want more. But we must fight that urge. Greed is never-ending, just like the concept of self-actualization. You get satisfied momentarily, but then you want to go higher. Once you do, you want to go even higher. I want to address this unveiled problem so that people understand how dangerous it can be to start running on a treadmill that can suddenly accelerate to a thousand miles speed without any warning.

Being Contented

Let us not forget the second part of the statement 'fulfillment and **contentment**.' Once you have achieved whatever it is that will make you feel content, you'll only be at a high for a short period of time, and soon your satisfaction will drop as you'd want to achieve something else. Now you're motivated to go higher, ignoring that God helped you get where you are. This is why contentment is important. Not being happy with what you've just achieved is the same as being ungrateful. This doesn't mean you should stop aiming higher. It just means you should never forget your past and always be happy with your present. If you suddenly hit a dead end, this is the point where you need to be the most content with your previously fulfilled objectives. God will get you through it.

I want to point out that I might have started off this chapter in a bit of a pessimistic tone, but it was needed to set the right approach. Many have chosen their path to fulfillment and have found their fair reward for following it. Those who have veered off their path have continued to hit roadblocks, detours, and speed bumps, in the end, realizing that they are on a never-ending cycle of going nowhere. Diversion from the *"I can't"* path will soon lead you to achieve much more in life. The ability to accomplish your desired goals is a real possibility. I have always told myself that I choose to be inspired by positivity and destined to make a difference. That positive attitude is, without a doubt, extremely important. A positive outlook on life can change an individual's life choices and hence lead to healthy self-awareness, social mobility, and spiritual enlightenment.

If you want to bring change into your own life or others' lives on a broader scale, you have to do it because doing nothing will not help. Whatever you feel will make you feel more fulfilled, *just do it*! Now I feel like I was sponsored by Nike or something! The point is, once you've decided what would make you feel fulfilled, don't shy away from it. You got this. Never stop until you complete it. One of my goals was to always surround myself with encouraging people, not superficial ones. It is essentially needed to achieve self-fulfillment. As I said earlier, once you know that this is what makes you feel happy and you know it will make the Lord happy, there is literally no other reason you shouldn't do what you aspire to.

Staying Strong

Sometimes you might feel intimidated by others' success, and that will downplay everything you try to do, but you have to hold on. Comparing your progress, mindset, or your idea with others is not very helpful. It would help if you only compare yourself to others for the sole purpose of learning. Comparison or competition can end up being unhealthy, or worse, detrimental to your psychological well-being. I chose to be true to myself, avoid comparing myself to others, and stay on the path of endurance until I am six feet under and unable to continue my journey any further. I have learned to *"Trust the Lord with all my heart, and lean not unto my understanding; in all my ways acknowledge Him, and he shall direct my path"* Proverbs 3:4.

I had a hard time trusting myself. I used to doubt my abilities and talents because I never looked at myself the way I do now. I had to lean on someone bigger than myself, someone who could see the bigger picture and who could get it done; the Lord. When I started to trust God more, I realized my abilities and talents. I never knew I was capable of certain things, but then I found out. Trying to strengthen your relationship with God will help you see that a life apart from him is impossible. He is a confidant and a friend who sticks closer than a brother. You know what you're doing is right, and that's more than enough. You know that you're doing something for God, and He will never let you down.

You will definitely meet some people in your journey that will attempt to hinder your growth and oppress you because they don't want to see you succeed. It's a fact; you'll meet many of these people, so be ready for them. Those people are what I call *blockers.* I term them that because they don't have your best interest at hand and couldn't care less about your future. Run from these people as fast as your little legs can carry you and never look back! Avoiding such people is crucial to your personal growth, for these people will stunt your growth with their harsh words and negativity.

Sometimes we find that we can't escape the belittling, discouraging microaggressions of life. There could be struggles with insecurity, worthlessness, and feel like a nobody because life has seemed so unkind. We always have better alternatives if we just search for them and get out of our own way. You have to surround yourself with encouragers and not discouragers. I know that no one likes to be alone, but if the person or people you are around can't see your best, then what's the point? No matter how negative they are? No matter how negative they are, being around them is embedded in the human psyche.

People want someone to call a friend, even if they clearly know these negative people don't care at all. These people are NOT your friends and do NOT have your best interest at hand. If you are finding it hard to get away from the unhealthy criticisms, then begin by slowly pulling away. Write daily affirmations for yourself to remind you that you deserve better, even if you don't think so yourself.

Affirmations Matter

Now in the last part of this chapter, I want to talk about affirmations. As I mentioned above, you could write too. Journal your affirmations, or you could take mental notes. The main point is to live by the affirmation. It could be as simple as telling yourself that you are doing great or understanding that the recent turn of events was by God's will and that you can still accomplish your goals because you have God by your side.

The common theme is acceptance. To accept that such is the situation and then look at your competencies and counter the problem with your immensely positive orientation and hard-working ethic. Affirmations have many advantages. Most importantly, an affirmation would greatly motivate you to achieve your aspirations or self-fulfillment objectives. Similarly, just going through your affirmation in your head or in your notebook would remind you of where you want to be, hence retaining a sense of direction and relevance.

This is your journey, not anyone else's. You'll have to walk the plank and swim with the sharks if you fall and find land somehow. Remember, you're not alone. You never are.

You have the only one you will ever need right above you. Just focus and run your course. As mentioned earlier, affirmations are declarations to remind yourself of how important and amazing you are. Many people would actually actively try to avoid writing affirmations about themselves because they aren't really confident in or happy about themselves. Writing your affirmation is the first step; once you take it, you'd realize how much you had been missing out on.

When you don't feel the best about yourself, this is the time to reflect on who you really are. This is the time when you need those affirmations. The way you see yourself is the way others see you. Simply put, if you are confident, happy, and contented about yourself, that is the exact impression others around you will receive. On the other hand, if you appear to sulk, be depressed, and desolate, people will see it. Most of them will try to avoid making contact with you in fear of catching that negative vibe from you.

The bottom line is that you have the power. Affirmations are just words that reinforce your true graceful personality. You have the power to attract whatever it is you want from life. Take the time to write one to three affirmations daily as a way to combat a self-defeating thought process. I promise you, you will not regret writing these, and you will not run out of affirmations or good things to write about yourself either.

I have added an affirmation chart below, which has the space to write three affirmations daily for a week. So whichever day you read this chapter... let's suppose it's a Tuesday. Write down three affirmations in the space given under 'Tuesday.' Repeat daily for the next six days. If you manage to do one week's worth of affirmations, you can get a journal and continue on that. Also, vision boards are a great way to motivate you to complete your goals and dreams. Scrapbooking is also beneficial as it promotes relaxation, optimism and will help with memory, as well as other therapeutic benefits.

Sunday

_____

_____

_____

Monday

_____

_____

_____

Tuesday

_____

_____

_____

Wednesday

_____

_____

_____

Thursday

_____

_____

_____

Friday

_____

_____

_____

Saturday

_____

_____

_____

Chapter 3: Don't Give Up

No Means, No!

Every time the word 'no' is presented to you, don't fall for it. It takes time to gain the ability to fight back against the blockers, but when you do, none can defeat you. It's a gradual process as you stab each *no* with a *who asked* you, but eventually, you'll develop the knack for it.

You have to teach yourself to go against the tide and try out things you never did. Here, I want to address a certain misconception people have about 'trying out new things.' Suppose you tell someone that you decided on a strategy to go out of your comfort zone to try out new things. Yes, people might look at you a little strangely. You might even be misunderstood or made to feel you are crazy for trying.

This new self you're trying to find could, for example, involve taking Taekwondo classes, hiking, climbing Mount Everest, or taking whatever challenge you wish to take on. Both these actions are not wrong or illegal, morally or religiously, yet they are potentially a new habit or experience you want to have fun with. They are doing what makes them feel happy, and you should do what makes you feel happy. If you genuinely enjoy something, you will have the drive to get there somehow, and eventually, undoubtedly, you'll get there. Persistence is key.

If I had a dollar for every time people told me 'NO,' I would be a millionaire. The support from family and friends around you doesn't help if you're told 'no' by many others. Keep in mind; many people do not have a supportive family or friends. If you do, consider it a blessing. Having supportive loved ones boosts your morale and drive to get where you want because you wouldn't be fearful of what, for example, your family would say. I understand that we have to ignore the voices of negativity, and even that, sometimes, doesn't work. You might be unable to ignore it all. I can tell you something that might make you feel a little bit better. Know that a demotion in this life is a promotion in the view of God.

Open Those Doors, Will You!

When life keeps closing the window of opportunity, and it will just remember it doesn't stay closed forever. Wait for your moment, just like a leopard waits patiently, analyzing their prey and only pouncing at the perfect moment. Just don't pass out for multiple hours like the leopard does because that burst of high speed makes them exceptionally tired yet tremendously fast! Even while that door is closed, try to find the other three just opened because of the former door shutting. There are always new opportunities that are unlocked; you just need to find them.

Another way to look at this is to believe that humans have a God-given gift to make their own opportunities. When it appears the thing you were pursuing fails, go for the next best alternative. Talk and tell people you trust about whatever has happened and ask them for their advice. They could help you out by recommending you to apply to some other college, workplace, or whatever it is that you want to do.

However, keep in mind to go for your first preference with every ounce in you, and if that, unfortunately, doesn't work out, then only do you work toward the second alternative. The last thing you want is to shut that door yourself by being too lazy to follow along with it. When there are obstacles in your way, stay resolute, and remember that obstacles are not obstacles at all. The obstacles that you face are building blocks to a higher calling in your life. Pile those closed doors on top of each other, and you'll start to gain a view of doors you never knew existed.

You have to see yourself serving your purpose and imagine yourself living it and accomplishing it. When you imagine yourself in the position you aspire to be, you'll experience more motivation to achieve your objective. Do not allow anyone or anything to stop you, and don't make excuses for why you can't achieve your goals. Excuses are immovable mountains that hinder you from seeing your true purpose in life.

Mom, I Think I Might Be Weird!

'I can't because people will judge me.'

'I look so weird.'

'I will look like a fool.'

Something I want you to note here is that weirdness is a subjective concept. You think you look weird because society places this stamp on you. Forget what society thinks, and you'll see your whole perspective on what to wear, how to style your hair, how to behave in certain places, how to interact with certain people; it will change you completely. Peculiarity varies cross-culturally. If you feel like people are rude or unaccepting toward you, get a flight and buy an island in the middle of the Pacific! Obviously, that's impossible for most people. What you can do is to determine your own personality and stick to what you feel is within the boundaries of your own moral compass and your religious principles.

Yes, the sting of regret can have a perpetual pain around your heart, and it might seem too immeasurable to escape. However, there is a way to harness regret by actively reaffirming that you are more than a simple 'no.' You are more powerful than just to self-destruct after being told that you are off. You are showing your weakness. A weakness you don't have. You will be strong when you think of yourself as strong. I am positive you've heard the common saying, *'you become what you believe.'* The meaning behind it is to recognize the power of your thoughts. If you believe you cannot make it, then you won't. It's about self-confidence.

Contrary to everything I've said above in this chapter, it's important to understand that sometimes a 'no' can prove to be a good thing. I am thankful for some of the 'no's I received in life. In retrospect, had I received a 'yes' that could have been the wrong direction for me, I could have missed a blessing in disguise. Living a life of trepidation will keep you stagnant. I learned this the hard way, but it's made me even more determined not to give up on my dreams, no matter what it took. I was going to rise above the mud and mire of defeat. It didn't matter to me that I was a divorcee raising two children alone and only having a high school education. You see, I was determined to make their lives better than the life I had established for myself. I refuse to allow anyone or anything to hold me back from my dreams in life.

Barging Through the Barriers

'I will not be silenced anymore and will live the life God predestined and preordained me to live.' I told myself.

Remember, no excuses and no regrets. Just because I only had a high school education, it didn't mean I couldn't achieve my heart's desires. It didn't mean I couldn't attain or obtain more in life. Though it was still true that I could attain and obtain more if I furthered my education and pushed myself toward a higher goal. I had to change my mindset and reeducate myself on what it was that I wanted. You can either make the worse of a situation or the best, but it's always up to you to change the trajectory set before you; life is what you make it, as I've said earlier. It's about your attitude toward it.

If you start to feel the preclusion of your life's journey is a continuous theme, then that's the time to recalibrate. That's the time to step out of your comfort zone and get creative. How many times have you repeated this narrative in your mind, *"It's just no use; things will never change"*? How often has your situation changed each time you told yourself repeatedly, in your mind, "it's *just no use; things will never change"*?

You begin to live in a state of inertia, and before you know it, the time has played a cruel joke on you and given you a timestamp that says, "Times Up." Don't give up or stop in the first place.

You are more valuable and needed than you think. There is a plan for your life, and we all know that life can give you a real swift kick sometimes. My suggestion; kick back and hard! It is easier to give up than to press ahead toward the prize waiting for you. Believe me, I KNOW!

I want to let you in on a little secret. I wish that when I was old enough to understand that someone would have told me that life is not fair. Had I known how unfair life could be, I would have planned my life differently to prepare for the twists and turns that came my way. Nevertheless, I went through life somewhat bright-eyed and bushy-tailed and didn't make the best decisions, so there were setbacks. There is nothing wrong with being eager and excited about what life can hold and opening yourself to new discoveries.

What is the very first thing you do when you wake up? The first thing I do is open my eyes, and then I begin deciding what to do next. Life is short, and tomorrow is not promised, so we must live each day like it's our last. Get off of the tightrope of impossibilities and soar to the possibilities life has for you. Believe it, see it, achieve it, and finish the race set before you. In Ecclesiastes 9:11, it is said that *"I have seen something else under the sun: The race is not to the swift or the battle to the strong, nor does food come to the wise or wealth to the brilliant or favor to the learned; but time and chance happen to them all."*

When I gave birth to my baby girl and held her in my arms, it was the proudest moment in my life. The pain I experienced during birth was excruciating, but that would not keep me from wanting another child. However, I was unsure if I could handle the throes of parenting. The question I posed to my doctor was if she could perform a tubal ligation because I didn't plan to have any more children. The doctor told me at the time I was too young, and she would not be able to accommodate my request. I wasn't sure how I felt at the time about her decision, but looking back, I'm glad she didn't honor my request. A few years later, I decided to have another baby. I was very sure that I was ready to conceive again, and I prayed to God for a baby boy. This time, my decision was final, and once again, I asked the doctor to perform the tubal ligation. The doctor obligingly honored my request and performed the procedure immediately after the birth of my son.

Many years ago, God had told me that I would have a child with mental illness years before I would decide to marry and have children. However, I ignored this as some kind of fleeting thought that was fear-based. The nagging thought never went away, and somewhere in my mind, I knew it would be a boy and that God had honored my prayers. I tried to escape the truth because I didn't want to deal with a child who had mental issues. God knew I would try to run from what he told me he would require of me. He told me he would require something of me and that to whom much is given, much is required. I had forgotten all about the nagging thought and asked God for the very thing I was afraid of.

God has sustained me through every mental outburst, profanity, and mixed emotions my son has at times. There are times when I don't recognize who he is. But then there are days when he is loving and funny. Such days have become one of my fondest memories. I know now that when God tells you something, accept it and believe it. Pray about it and ask for strength to endure whatever it is he has set before you.

I remember my son was graduating in the summer of 2007 and moving on to the next phase of his life. I can remember that day so clearly as he was leaving the 8th grade and beginning a new path to High School. I shouted out to him, "Sky's The Limit!" I had such expectations for him and wanted to help him reach his full potential, no matter what. There was so much hope and desire to see him to the finish line of his life journey. However, there would be a road less traveled as he would become diagnosed with schizoaffective disorder.

My World was shattered, and everything around me became dark, a tunnel with no light at the end. The years have been challenging, and I wish I could say that each day gets better, but it doesn't. However, I hold on to the promises of God and confidently know that he who began a good work in my son and me will continue to complete it until it's all said and done (Philippians 1:6).

Use the cards that you have been dealt more wisely and use them to your best advantage. When the valleys of despair close in on you, rise up and tell yourself it's not over. I will overcome this setback in life and continue my race to win the prize waiting for me. You are valuable. You are loved. You are YOU and can make the best or worst of your situation. Use the cards you're dealt with more wisely and use them to your advantage.

I haven't given up on my son, and I still pray for him every day and believe in the power of healing. If he never gets well and never becomes the son I once remembered, then that's okay because that is God's decision too. No matter what the outcome for his life is, I love him just the same and will continue to follow the path set before me, and no person or thing can stop me.

Chapter 4: Hamster Wheel

I'm sure you've seen a hamster wheel at some point in your life, maybe at a friend's place, in a film, or somewhere on the internet. You would have dismissed it as just an activity for a hamster, something to keep the pet busy. This wheel is more than merely a squished round cylinder. 'Hamster-wheel' is not a very common word, but it has a great deal of symbolic significance.

Symbolic Significance

A hamster wheel can symbolize some of the major issues we, as the human race, are experiencing. A vertically rotating structure with a basic circular movement function at face value, but to someone viewing it from an intellectual eye and making analogical connections reveals much more. A hamster wheel can be associated with monotony, nonfulfillment, lack of progression, and repetition, some of the problems most people are faced with on a regular basis.

Unwinding from the complexities of human life is increasingly becoming impossibly difficult. As societies are structured around competition and mon-making, and media is meant to reproduce a conspicuous consumption culture, individuals cannot simply exit their workplace one-day, thinking everything will be just alright. We are on a perpetual wheel of discontentment and trying to keep our sanity in the midst of it all. You could say that humans are like rodents, which are kept as pets, and the wheel is life.

All it wants to do is complete around on the wheel, but that's not a possibility. We are on the perpetual wheel like the rodent going round and round. The task is to run, and to run is the task. Literally, that is all the rodents can do. There's monotony, and then there is more monotony. There is no or limited progress, either. You get a job as a clerk, and it can potentially take you many years before you get to a favorable position. This can be seen in the case of a hard-working, competitive workaholic. Someone who didn't leave a law-firm to start from scratch at another.

No Escape

Another important aspect to look at is the level of satisfaction individuals achieve through work. When you ask them, many people will reply with a 'no' to the question, *"do you like your job?"* This becomes a problem because when these people come back home, they feel irritated and annoyed. This results in them shouting at their partner and children, the individuals in the closest proximity.

Unfulfilling activities of any type make the rest of their day unfulfilling as well. For example, if you don't want to work in the garden, your spouse insists on doing so aggressively. You'll do the work, but you won't enjoy it at all. This is a sort of unfulfilling activity that has the potential to make the rest of your day unfulfilling as well. Your life may become miserable, and, eventually, you will want to end your worries and find a safe haven from all that is slowly consuming your happiness and health. It's not as easy as it sounds, though. Once your hamster wheel is rotating at exceptionally high speeds, you cannot extract yourself from that wheel without hurting yourself or the others around you, psychologically or physically.

Wheel of Wellness

Now I want to bring in a concept that can tremendously help you. This can literally be the point at which you turn your whole life around, i.e., if you understand and apply it effectively to your life. *The Wheel of Wellness* is a diagram developed by Meyers, J.E., Sweeney, T.J., Witmer, J.M (1991) that includes the seven dimensions of your individual wellness. Balancing your life in these seven dimensions is the key to a healthy, well-rounded, and happy lifestyle.

In order to see the magic of this technique, you must take it in and apply it to whatever this is to life. Simply put, you need to replace your current ideological worldview with one that is balanced in the main seven aspects of human life. My recommendation to all readers is that they should try this out, even if it is just for two days or a week. You will see a visible difference. I am aware that the way I am talking about it makes it seem too good to be true; you might think I am exaggerating, but really I am not. This will work; you just need to believe it will, and you have to grasp the concept to the core and apply it appropriately.

The following are the seven dimensions and what each of them includes:

1- Spiritual well-being: involves understanding and becoming better aware of the beliefs, ideas, and ideologies found around you. For example, searching through the different beliefs and cultures and educating yourself on the religious knowledge that not many know of, and trying to find what gives your soul happiness and peace are some of the inclusions.

2- Emotional well-being: this includes the maintenance and appropriate handling of your emotions. A person who is unable to handle their anger or someone who is prone to spiraling down the dark roads of emotional instability is an example of not being emotionally well.

3- Intellectual well-being: this one is solely focused on the pursuit of knowledge. So any activity, which involves educating yourself academically or professionally. Anything that fosters your growth toward a state of higher intelligence and problem-solving ability contributes to this.

4- Physical well-being: there are two aspects to being physically well. One is to consume, and the other is to exert. The former requires a balanced, highly nutritious diet, and the latter, exercise to keep all your body up and running.

5- Social well-being: this involves engaging in a social activity that is healthy and progressively improving one's self. Toxic relationships, getting involved in unnecessary drama and wasting time with people who are taking you lower down the moral scale contribute to reducing social well-being.

6- Environmental well-being: as the name suggests, this involves being aware and taking care of the physical environment. Cleaning your room, engaging in volunteering activities and recycling trash are some actions that help you reach a state of higher environmental well-being.

7- Financial well-being: this includes keeping a lookout for your cash flow. It would be best if you planned out your consumption and earning patterns, keep records, pay on time, and avoid wasting unnecessarily. This all maintains your financial well-being.

Conclusion

All seven of these contribute together to make up your *individual wellness*. It is alright not to have perfect control over all seven. In fact, at the start of your venture, if you do choose to undertake this journey toward higher well-being, you might not have much grip over any of the seven. Things take time, and you should recognize that. Usually, some individuals perform better in some aspects than others. This is influenced by their identity, upbringing, culture, and the type of people they are connected to. For example, anyone might have higher financial well-being, but this does not guarantee that this person will do well physically or environmentally.

My suggestion would be that you print out a wheel of wellness, which you should easily be able to find online, or you could just make a circle with seven portions and write the seven dimensions of individual welling being within them. The concept is extremely simple, but obviously, the application requires quite a bit of focus and determination.

If you fancy this whole idea, you should definitely look up more resources and concepts linked to it. You can easily find alternative and complimenting ideas that should help you better understand this. Conclusively, use techniques and advice to help you unwind yourself from the hamster wheel you are undoubtedly stuck in; everyone is, only to varying degrees. Identify your problems and find a way to improve your lifestyle, making it healthier. The Wellness wheel is only one method.

Chapter 5: The Blame Game

Oh no! It happened again, didn't it? For the one-millionth time this month, something unfavorable has happened. Now what? Humans are bound to make mistakes and experience the fallout of their mistakes as well as the fallout following the actions of others. Consequences and dealing with them are characteristics of normal human life.

Fallouts

Fallout is the experience you have to undergo after some sort of action. In simpler words, a fallout is a reaction to an action. In this context, I'm referring to it with a negative connotation as the word is adverse in nature. There are three types: Internally-caused fallouts, Externally-caused ones, and the Supernaturally-caused.

As the name suggests, internally-caused fallouts are what you have to experience because of your own (internal) actions. An example of this type is if you're at the gas station getting gas and become angry about something, and in your anger, you pull off with the nozzle still in the tank. Your anger resulted in you having undesirable consequences.

The second type is preceded by actions that some other individual other than you did. As a result, you have to face the fallout. This also includes the time when someone reacts to your action, and their reaction causes a fallout for you. You playfully throwing a pillow at your sibling, making them react by throwing a wooden box nearby at you is a perfect example of an externally-caused fallout. You'll now have to deal with the injury, which is the fallout.

Thirdly, supernaturally-caused fallouts are a product of God. They are caused when God determines that you, as the individual, should experience any certain thing. An example of this would be when Jonah refused to obey God and go to the city of Nineveh to preach the gospel. As a result of his disobedience and trying to escape, he was swallowed up by a whale that eventually spewed him out on the Nineveh city's grounds.

An alternative way to understand this is through the origin of the action that precedes the fallout. So, in an internally-caused fallout, you, as the individual, do the action that causes the fallout. In an externally-caused fallout, it is some individual, other than you, who behaves in a certain way that results in you taking the fallout and, lastly, in a supernaturally-caused one, it is God who shifts the situation to be in a certain way, so you have to experience the fallout.

The Internal Reasoning

Bringing back our topic, when we face the fallouts, in our shock and helpless mental state, we blame it on someone or something. This is something every human does, and many do it to the extent where they don't even realize they are playing the blame game. A classic setting for the blame game is in failures. When you are hit with a failure, you search desperately for the cause. You want a reason behind it.

Life always has a cause and effect formula. I failed the test because I didn't study. I did not get the job because I was too nervous during the interview. My kids are rude because they got the wrong company in school. We had a divorce because my partner failed to find a middle-ground with me. I had an accident because the other driver zoomed past the red traffic light and hit my car. I feel sick because I ate something I knew I was allergic to. This list can go on forever because there are unlimited combinations of causes and effects.

In essence, humans need a cause for every effect. When they don't find one or when they see that the cause is they themselves or a beloved person, they put the blame on something else. You could say that the world of the average human starts to crumble without the stability that the cause and effect formula brings.

Disadvantages
Growth Stagnation

This is the biggest and fastest surfacing problem of playing the blame game. Growth requires one extremely important element, which is to realize our mistakes and to move past them. When we don't recognize our mistakes and learn from them, we cease to move forward. However, realizing our mistakes and learning from them stops the repetitious cycle. Growth begins, and the major steps of denial can be a thing of the past.

Unacceptance of Faults

When we don't accept the faults in our lives and keep on blaming others, we'll start to develop this ideology of stubbornness, i.e., accepting your incompetency. You will find it difficult to say *"Yes, it's my fault"* or *"I did it"* because you will be so accustomed to throwing the blame around.

Dissatisfaction from Others

as a result of you blaming others, you'll start to see them in a negative light. Yes, it could be their fault, but in most cases, it's combined with your own fault to produce the fallout that you had to experience. This dissatisfaction and disappointment from others are likely to make you distrustful of others and even cut your ties with friends and family.

Unrealistic Familiarization

Lastly, an important part of unrealistic expectations you place on yourself or others is that you are making their lives difficult as well as your own. Give yourself room to breathe and others, room to make mistakes. Familiarity sometimes breeds contempt. We can become too comfortable and too familiar with those close to us and feel that gives us a license to blame and point fingers. Every person has their own flaws, and we should not take up time focusing on them. Rather, we need to look at our own flaws. We should often question ourselves about how we can change for the better and become the best version of ourselves.

Resolution

You may not be able to change your past, but you can change your present and future situation. Whether that change is for good or bad is up to you. You can't blame anyone for your past, present, or future outcome. The only person you can blame is yourself if you choose not to do anything about it. There might be a lot of people you want to blame, but it does no good and only holds you back from moving forward.

Learning to focus on what I have to do to make change possible is the difference between sitting in the stands and doing nothing or getting out there in the field and playing the game. I know life is not fair at times, and there can be so many disappointments. You want to give up and give in, but you continue to push forward past the obstacles of life. Trying to stay positive is never easy in the midst of your trials. Remember, there are those watching you to see how you handle the pressure. They will have to face the same pressures in life one day, and you just might be the person they look up to for guidance.

Don't be afraid to follow your dreams or dream big. Choosing to focus on me and not what the outside world thought of me took some readjusting in my thought process.

I had to realize that the only thing that matters is what God thinks of me and what I think of myself. I was trying so hard to please everyone and do what they wanted me to do and lost myself in the process. A little late in the process, but better late than never. Whatever it is you want to achieve in life, just go for it. What do you have to lose?

There is this old saying by Theodore Roosevelt that goes: *"Nothing Worth Having Comes Easy."* You might feel like you are swimming against the tides of life. You feel you're getting closer to achieving your goal, a wave comes and pushes you back further, and you have to begin again. That wave could be sickness, homelessness, joblessness, family, friends, finances, death, or you. You could be holding yourself back because you won't try. What I have learned to do is to ride the wave, ride the wave until you can't ride it anymore.

You may have to ride it crying, angry, delusional, or sometimes alone. My feelings have been a combination of all those emotions, yet optimism continues to reign in my heart, mind, and soul. *"Yet this I call to mind and therefore I have hope: Because of the Lord's great love we are not consumed, for His compassions never fails. They are new every morning; great is Your faithfulness."* Lamentations 3:21–23

Chapter 6: Stand Firm

When you've had many tests and trials, seemingly more than you can bear, but presently your soul is flooded with peace and serenity in just knowing Jesus, your burdens he will bear.

When all things around you start to crumble, and floods of life bring much despair, but oh! The joy and comfort of knowing that Jesus Christ the Savior cares.

Then all around you, light shines brighter day and night the same because can't no woe nor foe detain him from coming to the saints calling on his name.

For he has promised to be with us in trouble, to be our refuge, our stronghold, a firm foundation that cannot be shaken, a rock of defense that cannot be moved.

Oh! Take and let his words possess you, hold them precious in your heart and soul, they will ever give you peace and comfort as you trust by the faith in the Savior's Love.

A Poem by Gladys Ramsey

Poem Analyses

The above poem emphasizes the inevitability of trials and tribulations. There is an intense description of how problems can come flooding into your life. You imagine yourself standing in the middle of the flood, wondering what to do and hoping the waters will somehow dissipate. These trials and tribulations are piercing, and the intensity of frustrations penetrates your heart and mind. You feel physically and emotionally drained.

But then, suddenly, you'll feel as if all your problems are being lifted off your shoulder. This, according to the writer of the poem, is Jesus taking the burden of your problems upon himself. I think there is much comfort in just the thought of someone else taking up for you. Then there are also some words about how the Lord greatly cares for his servants. He would always extend His hand to pull us out of the darkness. Learn to stand firm against the avalanche of hurdles and complexities that will attempt to knock you out into the abyss of ungratefulness and depression.

The poem also speaks of the Lord's strength and how nothing or no one can change the fact that He is always there for us, to give us refuge in the shade of his magnificence. The poem ends with giving us the advice to turn to God for the solution to our problems. Specifically, it suggests we should 'let the words possess us.' By this, the writer means to say that one should surrender to the Lord;

subjugate yourself to him, and watch as all your entanglements uncurl themselves and leave you stress-free.

Be Firm

Amid your trials and tribulations, always remember who is in control and stand firm. Easier said than done, especially when there seems to be no light at the end of the tunnel. The demands of life are knocking at your door, the bills are piling up, and there is no remedy in sight. These trials and tribulations will come and go as long as we are on earth, but there is a way of escape. I will discuss this topic more in Chapter 8 on forgiveness and how God uses these trials to begin a healing process within.

Someone once shared with me some personal trials and tribulations they were going through. They just felt like giving up on life and giving in because nothing was going right. They began to explain to me how their hair was falling out. They were diagnosed with high blood pressure, prediabetes; they lost a job and a relationship—all this in 3 years. "Life sucks right now, and on top of all my issues, I have to go through it alone. I know there are other people with worse issues than mine or similar issues, but how am

I supposed to stay hopeful in the midst of failing health and joblessness".

My heart broke for this person, and I wasn't sure what I could say to comfort them. I knew that just having an ear to hear and allowing them to vent their concerns were somehow enough. They were correct in saying that life is unkind at times and can sometimes give us unfavorable life events. However, there is hope that makes us not ashamed, and that will provide us with the power to overcome every situation. I found that hope in Jesus Christ because of him; my strength is built.

"And hope maketh not ashamed; because the love of God is shed abroad in our hearts by the Holy Ghost which is given unto us." (Romans 5:5 King James Version)

When we feel pressed against the wall of despair, we must find a way to rise above our circumstances. She needed to change her mindset and begin to believe that she could have better health, know that she is not alone, and start a new course of discovery. Eventually, this person began to realize they weren't their situation and could begin making the necessary changes to become healthier and find reciprocal love.

The decision wasn't made overnight, and there were many days and nights of heartache. True, it takes time and perseverance to get the results we want, but the effort is worth it. Life goes on even when we feel it has stopped for us. The world will continue to spin on its axis, sunrise and sunset will continue, and the seasons will change. The decision is ultimately yours at the end of every day and how you choose to play a part in changing the trajectory of your life. I would tell you to try and choose wisely because you only get one life to live.

Begin to choose what is best for you and try to see what that would ultimately look like. Do you see yourself healthier, happier, and less stressed, or do you see yourself overwhelmed, unhappy, and just settling?

Guard Your Heart

Relating to all aspects of human life, always guard your heart. The heart has four chambers, upper and lower. These chambers have the responsibility to make sure blood flow is traveling in the right direction. The atria and ventricles are pumping and receiving the blood. These are only a few intricate details of what the heart does, and it's only the size of a fist. It is so important to protect the heart not only physically but spiritually and emotionally.

When we put unneeded angst on the heart, we are creating a recipe for disaster. The stressors of life, emotional up-setters, anger, un-forgiveness, and loss are detrimental to your heart's health. Harboring unhealthy emotions is never good, especially if you hold on to them for too long. If you feel that you are being taken advantage of or no one understands your pain, that's okay. There is a time to present your grievances and fight your cause when you have been wronged. You should be heard when a wrong has been done to you, and you continue to be treated unfairly.

You should never be treated like a doormat or like you are unimportant. There is so much to contend with in life, and you are only one person, so pick your battles carefully.

Chapter 7: Dig Deep

I know you're tired and feeling the cloud of despair settling around you. You just want things to work out; you just want to be happy, but there are so many complications barricading your way. Many think that people who're going through desolate and depressive times should be left alone. *"They just need some time to think about it."*

Desolation

It is true that people sometimes need time to think problems through, but many times things don't go as planned. There are two major reactions to desolation:

Prosperous Culmination

This is where individuals within the deepest and darkest depths of despair find a way out. They are able to look past their thoughts of regret or prideful ambitions that were once thought admirable. Feelings of sadness begin to become feelings of determination that prove to be helpful.

Self-Destructive Culmination

This is when the individual travels even deeper down and into the realm of ultimate despondency. The hopelessness they experience feels like a deep well that has swallowed them up, and the endless pain of negativity continues to swell up around them. Most of the time, it is a restrained version of self-destructive culmination that we see and feel. Occasionally, you might see an extreme case as well, but usually, people are saved before they plummet to this sort of dangerous state.

Opportunity

It is argued that people should be left to come to terms with their issues if they are experiencing desolation, but personally, I feel that this is actually the fitting time to dig deeper. By deeper, I mean, this is the time to access a level of your consciousness that you never knew existed. This is the time when one should try to bring that prosperous culmination from within you.

Without a doubt, the choices made and the behaviors demonstrated during the era of darkness are unmatchable to any other time of your life. These decisions made and behaviors expressed are, many times, adverse. What you can do is to take steps to reduce the chance of the adverse side from reigning dominant at the end of each day. I understand that it's impossibly difficult to appreciate and be grateful for your blessings at times when you feel the worst, but really, this is one effective strategy.

One suggestion I can give you is to keep a small notebook with you all day, keep it on your bedside or workplace desk if you can. In this notebook, make it a habit to write every blessing you can think of. At the start, you'll have much to write about, so maybe start on a weekend. This way, you have the time to fully write all the specific and detailed blessings to be grateful about. As you progress through your days, keep on adding to the list. You might literally never run out of blessings. Just looking at the list should make you feel privileged and give you the push that you need to exit the dark dimension.

Take your sadness as an opportunity instead of a weakness. Take it as a blessing in disguise to uncover the blessings that you have neglected for so long. When you're in the race and your feet are bleeding, your body is aching, your mind is flooded with doubt, and you can't see the end of the race, just keep on believing. I feel many people revert to hopelessness merely hours before something amazing is about to happen to them.

God loves each and every one of us; you need to brand that into your head. God is only testing you because he loves you and wants you to develop into the best version of yourself, and in order to do so, you need to experience situations that trigger your self-development muscles. Think of it this way. You are like a seed in the earth. You are simply there, simply existing. There is no more to your existence than being embedded into the soil.

Then God tests you. Think of those tests as water. That water gradually seeps through the layers and finally arrives around you. However, you wouldn't instantaneously turn into a large plant the second that water touches you. It will take some time, but then you'll start to see it for yourself. You'll feel the tiny leaves trying to spurt from within you. Soon after, you'll have a stem stemming from the ground, and you'll have the greenest of leaves. You just need to have patience.

Just know that if you keep going you can reach the end and the prize is waiting there for you. If you don't start in the first place, if you don't fight against your inner demons as well as the outer ones, you'll never get to the finish line. This is the time when you have to dig deep and push yourself. Tell yourself that the race is not over and that it is just inaugurating; this is just the beginning.

I'm tired, I am exhausted, I just can't do it, everything around me is falling apart, and nothing is working out right for me. Everyone else around me seems to be doing fine, and they can do it, then why can't I? What is wrong with me, and why am I always neglected, rejected, and ignored? You have to stop listening to the self-doubt and replace those thoughts with positive reinforcements, and believe in yourself. Everyone knows that before you finish a race, you have to be in one.

At the beginning of the race, there is a starting point, and at that point, there is an adrenaline rush throughout your body. You are ready to surpass your opponent and finish with success at any and every cost. However, you are ready to give up when in a second, minute, hour, day, week, or year, your prize was there waiting for you, but you GAVE UP too soon. Don't stop; forge ahead and do what you were initially called to do in life; your purpose and potential, achieve it. Accept and keep in mind that you might not always win the race, but your fortitude withstood the challenge.

If you don't get what you want, I guarantee you that you won't be disappointed in yourself. You won't be disappointed because at least you tried, you stepped out on faith and tried to make a difference, and that's what counts. This effort is what God actually sees. We are not going to always see the changes that we make in everyone's life, and we won't always know who we have positively influenced.

"Not only so, but we also glory in our sufferings, because we know that suffering produces perseverance; perseverance, character; and character, hope. And hope does not put us to shame, because God's love has been poured out into our hearts through the Holy Spirit, who has been given to us" Romans 5:3-5.

In Light of Personalized Retrospect

There have been many times when I felt like giving up, more times than I can count. I felt like giving up when my son was diagnosed with a mental disorder, when my dad tragically died, when I got a divorce, when I lost my job and when I fell into serious depression. I just didn't want to go on with life. I wanted an end to it all.

I remember telling God that I just didn't want to see another day; this is the extent to which it had gone. Now that I look at it, it saddens me to think about how bad things had gone just because of losing hope. But did God listen to my depressive request? Thank God he did not! I asked for something I should have never, but at that time, it seemed like the only way out.

I'm so glad he didn't listen to me. I didn't want to see the light shine through the window like I normally did every morning. I wanted to block everything and everyone out of my life. I lost whatever purpose and direction I had. That day, for some unexpected reason, God spoke to me. The second I opened my eyes, the verse *"My Grace Is Sufficient"* (2 Corinthians 12:9) was echoing through my head. He spoke those words to me before any other thought could enter my mind. He spoke to me before I could say anything or think of anything. He told me how his grace was sufficient.

Those words activated something inside me as if it was a light-switch inside me that had been off and undiscovered till this point in my life. The Lord's words had now switched it on. I knew there was something more in my life. I knew then that I had to go on because he had something for me to complete, and he wasn't done with me yet. He has something in store for everyone. You just need to connect to him through prayer and have a thirst for knowledge to find out what he has for you

Chapter 8: Forgive Yourself

It's intrinsically human nature to make mistakes, and every individual has to understand that. If you really believe that it's possible to live an almost flawless life, your belief is flawed! Humans and blunders go hand in hand throughout your life. Accepting that mistakes will happen is the beginning of realizing you are not perfect, but you're doing awesome things in spite of your imperfections.

You could have smiled at someone on the subway, did some charity, made your partner something that they thoroughly enjoyed, or you might have made your friend laugh really hard. Many do not understand that even the smallest deeds that might not even overtly seem like deeds in the first place can contribute to making you a great person whom God loves, and people enjoy the company of.

Now that we've established the inevitability of slip-ups let's move on to how to deal with them. This chapter will mostly focus on self-forgiveness.

Sometimes the appropriate outcome is what exactly you get, and at other times the outcome might be disastrous. When you don't get the outcome you desired, pray, and seek another solution to the problem and repeat the process until you get the expected result. Kicking furniture, punching walls, and screaming into someone's ear works like a charm as well...just kidding! I am aware that we want to stop time and just scream and throw a tantrum, which may have crossed your mind from time to time, but that is not the solution. When you can find quiet time, use it, take advantage of every opportunity to self-evaluate, meditate, and restructure your thought process about yourself and life in general.

People can do a great job of beating themselves up with self-doubt and unworthiness. However, what's the point? Reassurance is the best teacher because it would help you realize that one step at a time is all one has the ability to do. The frustrations of trying to achieve one's ultimate goal can be debilitating, especially when it seems that none of your dreams are coming true and nothing appears to be working out for you. Seemingly, no one is listening to you or wants to listen to your heartfelt angst about your challenges.

You feel you cannot change anything, but that is untrue. Indeed, the past cannot be changed, but the present and future can. You can change your present and future situations at a moment's notice. Whether that change is for good or bad is up to you. You can't blame anyone for your past, present, or future outcome but you. Although there are a lot of people you may want to blame, it does no good and will only keep you from moving forward.

Learning to focus on what to do to make change possible is the difference between sitting in the stands or doing nothing. Nonetheless, continue to push forward and past the obstacles of life.

Importance of Self-Forgiveness
Fosters Growth

I believe that this is perhaps one of the more significant reasons why you should quit hating yourself. You saturate in your position when you overthink your mistakes, and that's the worst. As an individual, growth is crucial to your existence. You are meant to go out in the world and learn about it, the people within it, the experiences, and yourself.

In addition, instead of hating yourself for your mistakes, try to learn from them. If you forgot to pay someone who you loaned some money from, next time write it down somewhere, so you don't forget. It's quite simple; learn from mistakes.

Furthermore, trials and tribulations that one has to go through are from God so he can teach and help you grow. He wants us to be the best versions of ourselves that we possibly can. The only way this is possible is by placing you in situations and testing your patience, gratitude, emotions, and compassion. As a result of these incidents and experiences, we, as humans, are meant to learn and grow, not to cry about it in a corner or harm ourselves. Self-harm will be discussed in much detail a bit later on in this chapter.

Grants Focus

Because of the fact that you would have forgiven yourself, you would be ready to move on to other aspects of your life; the positive ones. The time saved from not thinking about your miseries can be translated to creativity. You can focus on polishing a skill that you might have. For example, if you have a knack for arts & crafts, you should focus all your free time and effort on it instead of thinking about how you talked slightly rudely to a lady on the elevator last Monday.

Now, don't get me wrong. I'm not saying that what you did is okay. All I am saying is that you need to forgive yourself for it. Yes, there is no doubt that you made a mistake, but now don't make another mistake by wasting your time over-thinking about it. Focus on something more productive.

Fuels Negativity

Another reason why self-forgiveness is important is that being in a negative headspace where all you think about is how you could have done so, which would have prevented the whole thing from happening. That's useless. What has been done has been done. Instead of killing yourself from the inside, you need to move on. If you do not, you will think of yourself as the worst person on the planet, and as a result of your negative view of yourself, you're quite likely to spew negativity and hate on those around you.

Your negativity radiates through you, and it affects others even if your intentions are completely the opposite of it. You have the ability to make someone cheerful or gloomy. The choice is yours. You can either forgive yourself, love yourself so you can live a happy, fulfilling life where those around you want to be around you. Or you can live a life of self-hate and negativity, where people avoid your company because they fear your adverse energy.

Develops empathy

Forgiving yourself for your wrongdoings helps you understand that mistakes happen; everyone makes them. When you're used to forgiving and overlooking your own mistakes, you're very likely to start forgiving others as well. This is because you start to realize that anyone can have a tongue slip in the heat of the moment. This breeds sympathy because you know that you might have reacted similarly, i.e., charged by emotions in someone else's place.

Improves Health

Because your health is psychologically proven to be directly proportional to your mental state. If you are unhappy with yourself about something that you did, your health suffers from it, both psychological and physiological. So you could say you're technically damaging your brain and body unintentionally in the process of crying over mistakes.

You'll see a clear difference in your health if you start forgiving yourself, and that's a fact. You will have better mental clarity, higher cognitive abilities, more energy in your body, better appetite, and improved workouts. It's like a burden on you has been lifted. Keep in mind that this is a burden that you have created yourself and have placed on your head yourself, so it's only you who can and should remove it. Forgive yourself and see for yourself.

Personal Experience

Being a single mother, I have suffered from serious self-doubt, self-loathing, and overthinking. We all make mistakes. I made mistakes, but there was an issue. Even when things were not my fault, I somehow continued to blame myself and began feeling even worse.

Being a single mom meant I was the only breadwinner, so I had to work tirelessly to provide my kids with a decent lifestyle. However, this also meant that I couldn't give them the time and the company any normal mother does. I felt as if I had failed my children and myself. God had bestowed upon me my kids as blessings, yet I was unable to play the role of a good mother. This is not just me; many single mothers feel similar to what I have.

Single motherhood can be a difficult position to be in, but you can reverse it around and make it a beautiful experience as well. Single mothers struggle due to multiple reasons, one of which is that the whole burden of income generation falls on their shoulders. For women who were housewives prior to their divorce or separation, this hits even worse as they are forced to find a job and adapt to a work culture in a short amount of time. Even if you have been working, the stress levels go ten times higher because you know that you won't be the best you can be for your children if you become terminally ill. There is a possibility that they will experience unfavorable circumstances because you cannot provide for them.

Furthermore, single motherhood is also frowned upon in many countries, and this adds an additional complication to the already complicated lifestyles of single mothers. The stigma is gradually being lifted, but some still undergo the stares and hurtful words. There is also the fear that children might experience a social, financial, and emotional problem. Children need their parents to be role models and guide them through difficult times. Having a parent, caregiver, teacher who can positively influence them on the right path is very important.

Every parent is enough for their kids, even if they are single. Stop believing in the lies and start considering yourself complete and enough for your kids. That's honestly the best advice you need.

Let me tell you; it was not a simple task to get out of that negative self-hating mindset. I felt my kids would be at a disadvantage in life because of my doings, while when I think about it now, my kids were just fine with me. They were happy with me; only I wasn't happy with myself. Stop thinking bad about yourself because you're doing your best.

Even if you fail to carry out your duties, always remember there is God to look out for you and your kids. You are worthy, and you are the best mom your kids could have. Make this your slogan, brand this into your conscious, and you'll only see yourself improve as a mother and as a human being.

Forgive yourself; move on from your desolated states. Forgive to forget. You'll be better off, I promise. Learn from your mistakes and avoid them in the future. And always remember that you are worthy of the best.

Chapter 9: Fear

Fear is a loop of unconscious persistence that keeps the soul from tasting the rightful freedom that lies beyond fright. There are always walls barricading the juicy bits of life. The best does not come easy. This chapter will mostly focus on the fear of failure rather than fear of ghosts, death, or clowns.

Reactions

When you are faced with a mountain to climb, a river to cross, a test to top, or an interview to ace, humans demonstrate three possible reactions.

Initiative hindrance – they do not even begin the journey because they just know that nothing will work. They seemingly foresee failures before even starting. This one shows the highest level of fear, laziness, or both, and hence the person who mostly denies opportunities this way needs to work a lot on himself or herself.

Midway abandonment – this is where they start their undertaken objective fully committed to succeeding. However, the further they go, their motivation levels drop.

Their determination to turn the dream into reality is lost over time, and they abandon their journey in the mid-way.

Hit-&-run approach – in this, they have already identified that they won't get anywhere. As a result, they only expend minimal resources just for the experience or a tiny gain. Motivation and determination are lost not long after. This one is focused more on luck because, as the name suggests, you hit and run, hoping that somehow your shot landed somewhere.

Drawbacks

Fear of failure does not have a single benefit, but its adversities are many. Some of the major ones are as follows:

1- Loss of opportunity: you never know which opportunity will be the one that takes you considerably further in life. Keep in mind that the opportunity could be more than financially beneficial. You could make connections that you might use some years down the line. Similarly, the experience of trying to achieve your desired goals can prove to be quite valuable.

Even if you fail, there is so much to learn from any and everything in this world. There is no physical value of experiences, but they have a great deal of significance and must not be ignored.

2- Reduced confidence: if you shy away once, you're very likely to do it again. The same goes for the opposite. If you do something beyond your comfort zone, you'll gain enough confidence to do it again. If there is one trait that you really need to develop and work on throughout your life, that is confidence. It can take you places otherwise impossible.

Confidence can be the difference between success and failure in many contexts, such as public speaking, making a presentation, interviews, or meeting someone for the first time. You do not want to be losing it to fear. Many people take a chance with an opportunity, and if they fail, they never ever want to take a chance again. This is a bad move; instead, you should learn from that failed attempt and apply the findings to the next experience.

3- Worsened future life chances: when you get used to ignoring opportunities, you'll miss out on social experiences and financial ventures that can improve your social mobility. This is because whoever presented you the opportunity might not again due to your disinterest in the first one.

4- Destroyed self-worth: when you want to achieve something but you fear failure too much, you'll overtime start to hate it and yourself. Your self-worth will decline as well because you know you are unconfident, and that can make you feel despondent.

Personal Case

I can remember many times that I would sabotage multiple opportunities for success. I cut off my own plans of success myself just through my fear of failure. If I felt as if I was getting close to my vision or special moment, fear gripped me the hardest and made me run away. I expressed my fear by making excuses or purposely messing it up for myself because I believed it could never work out for me.

The fear of failure or of what people would think of me was so overwhelming. My brain was always bombarded with feelings of remorse, guilt, and self-doubt. I would wonder if I could really accomplish what I wanted to. Eventually, I just gave-in to just being content with whatever life had to offer. Now, don't get me wrong. Being content is important, but the best way to go about it is by being achievement-oriented and being content.

Facing reality is very hard, and it is so easy to hide behind others' success or evade it altogether. How many times have you disembarked from your path to success? How many times have you journeyed on a course and then decided to detour completely? You're always feeding yourself this procrastinating drug.

"I need to first get done with high school, and then I'll start a small business. Oh, it's alright, college is to consume. I'll have my first start-up running by the end of college. I need to get a job first for a stable income. My relationship and work are weighing me down. I just need a break. Okay, I can't do this".

Initially, you might have felt that you would take the world by storm, but over time, you just thought it wasn't possible. The mere thought of attempting something started to cause fear and doubt to arise from deep within. When fear creeps up, talk to fear, and let fear know who is in charge of your destiny. It's not just you. Everyone has trouble with achieving their dreams. Everyone struggles with doing what they want.

Remember the end goal and what it is you're after. Find your safe place and release everything you are feeling related to fear or judgment there, and the next day, go back to achieving your goal. One crucial part of earning an achievement is finding support. Many times you might not be skilled or experienced at something. That is the time when you need someone to help you. Instead of feeling ashamed or thinking, the person will be annoyed by you, approach them, or someone you trust. Ask for their help. Explain everything and what you're going through.

If they are unable to help, ask them to refer someone. Never ever try to do something you do not know much about. Ask for help! No one loses dignity or respect from asking for help. You can also collaborate with others who are as passionate as you about what you're doing. Do everything in your power to make sure nothing that you can blame remains. No longer should you say it was so and so keeping me away from my hopes and aspirations!

You are a sophisticated human being with your own desires, interests, and expressions. You do not need anyone to limit you from achieving your true potential. Unfortunately, the bottom line to this is that you are that person. You are the person who is limiting you from being the person you want to be.

Who will you blame when others are helping you achieve your goals? This is why collaboration and seeking support help out. When there were no more negative accusations, doubts, or anyone saying "you can't," the only person now holding me back was me - only me, myself, and I.

"Okay, Rah! You have to face the truth and look at yourself and know without a doubt that things are possible." Being vulnerable in the face of adversity is never easy. If I keep running from what makes me feel uneasy and fearful, I will never move forward.

Resolution

A solution to any problem starts with its realization. First, you need to recognize that there is a problem and then identify the specific times or situations when and where it is prevalent. Accepting the problem is what prepares your body and mind before you try to solve the issue.

Secondly, I would like to bring your attention to the fact that the opportunities you might be presented with are not always workable and achievable realities. Understanding this is really important because if you think that everything will work out for you, there is always a chance of failure, but that does not mean you become desolate and never achieve anything ever again. Learning from failures is crucial in order to minimize the chances of failure next time.

Furthermore, as you keep pursuing whatever you are passionate about, you constantly learn and progress regardless of your failures or success. Keep in mind that progression doesn't necessarily have to be up the social scale. You will fail, know that. It's impossible for everything to work out flawlessly for you. Believing in this false truth is impractical.

Over time, after succeeding as well as failing, your intuition will start to develop. Why is this intuition important? Your intuition and experience will help you determine which opportunities you should have a go at and which don't seem to have a benefit at the end of the tunnel. This means you're likely to only invest your time, effort, or money in the projects that will prove to be beneficial.

As mentioned earlier, approaching others for help is very effective. There is nothing wrong with asking for help, and there should be no hesitation because your chances of succeeding in whatever venture you have undertaken are improved.

Lastly, if there is one solution to taking advantage of opportunities, it is focusing on confidence. The more confident you are in your predictions, yourself, and your abilities, the better. When you trust yourself and have a firm faith that God will help you make only the best choices, you are much more likely to achieve the best of the best. Have firm trust and jump in. Jump into the sea of opportunity. You will reign buoyant. Believe in yourself!

Chapter 10: Dying To Live Or Living Until I Die

Some people live their lives as if every day were their last while others gracefully go through life, confident as if tomorrow was promised to them forever. Similarly, some individuals adhere to the 'YOLO' way of life in which they believe one should do every possible thing because you might never get the chance to live that life ever again. YOLO stands for You Only Live Once.

You might have heard the term living on the edge. Some are engrossed in this way of life where they engage in dangerous, sometimes rebellious activities and extreme sports.

Why is there so much diversity in terms of the way people perceive life? Why do some people fear death to great extents whilst others' do not think twice before making an adverse leap of faith?

You can live your life in whatever way you choose; it is nobody's business. The crux of the situation is to live with purpose simply. That purpose of yours could be fulfilled in various ways, and the purpose itself largely varies from person to person. If you believe in God, he decides your purpose according to your capabilities and competencies.

He knows how much you can take and how much you can give, and so he does not over-burden you with a responsibility that is out of bounds for you. To a certain degree, humans are also allowed to determine their own paths of purpose.

If you do not believe in God, you solely determine your purpose by yourself through experiences that shape you and interactions that ignite that spark within you. That spark is the purpose. Maybe you experience a horrible incident involving animal abuse that could suddenly become your spark. Your purpose could now suddenly be to safeguard and shelter animals from harm. Even the tiniest of things can bring about your spark.

Every individual can have multiple purposes, some determined by God, while others decide for themselves.

The actuality of human life is, simply put, quite sad. It's sad because when we start growing up, multiple problems and complex aspects are thrown onto us that we do not know how to solve or understand. Some of us realize our abilities and our purposes in time, but unfortunately, many of us fail to do so. This can possibly cause us to live a life of confusion, despondency, depression, and unhappiness.

The purpose is crucial to the wellbeing of every individual of the human race. Without purpose, you are merely an entity that is breathing, interacting, and consuming, but not living, excelling, developing, or achieving. The mindless wandering throughout the years of life is destructive and unhealthy for the individual and those around them.

We only get one life to live, only one life to prove that we are worthy—one life to realize our potential. If you fail, that is it. There are no second chances in life. It is said that there are only five or six moments in an average human's life that they get the opportunity to determine whether they want to be the person that they want or the person that they would despise in the future. Five or six chances in a life span of 60 to 80 years isn't much, is it?. Moreover, some do not even get the chance to get there. Find your moments and do what is right. Find those moments and realign your life in the direction that will bring you the closest to your purpose.

Walk past regrets and bitterness; it should not be an option. I was faced with situations that could have settled me into a permanent state of regret. But, by the Grace of

God over time, I built up my defenses. I told myself, "*no way, no ma'am.*" Sure, at times, I would be bitter, angry, and regretful if I look at all the things that did not go my way, but when I really thought about it, it makes better sense to live with a grateful heart.

Each day there is an opportunity to start again. People think that you have lost all your progress when you start again, which can be the case sometimes. However, the experience you got from your attempt should not be underestimated. The second you try to conquer the same or similar thing, all that you learned from your previous attempt helps you charge forward with greater strength and effectiveness.

Every effort you put in for the betterment of society, yourself, your family, animals, organizations, and the environment, goes a long, long way, and even while you don't recognize it, it's actually taking a step closer toward fulfilling your life's purpose.

Take a minute right now, close your eyes, and think about your deepest regret in silence. Focus on it; what do you see? What thoughts run across your mind, and what do you feel when you think about it? Now take those feelings, thoughts, regrets and turn them into something that you never thought you could imagine.

Take that negativity and transform it into positive energy. It's the energy that will heal your psychological damage and brighten-up your perception of life. Make every hour on this planet a blessing to your soul, body, and mind, not an albatross of pain. You will discover that your moments of hurt and disappointment do not really have a hold on you; they are powerless against a healthy human.

People say that they can never be someone else because of the scar that they're past left on them. Yes, indeed, the past does affect you. But you have the choice to let that past wreak havoc on your future. The other option you have is to learn from the past and move on.

If you manage to control that abomination living inside you, you will be freed from the shackles of your failures, regrets, and negativity. You'll be able to breathe again and to see the world in a completely new way.

We all know that death is inevitable, and there is no escaping it. When, where, and how death will occur is unknown. However, when we are alive and well, what is the point of thinking of things that have happened in the past.

You do not have to waste your time thinking about the past as this would be an unproductive practice.

We are not meant to live to worry about how, when, and where; we simply just live for the purpose of living. If I spent my days worrying about such things, I would have never been able to live. Now, it's not as if I am not human, and these negative feelings haven't crossed my mind; it's just that I realized what I had to do. The feelings do crop up every now and then, and that is normal, but I do not allow them to dictate my existence.

I just hope that when my time is up, I will have made enough of a difference. A difference that allowed others to know that they are not alone, that you are not less than, and that you matter more than you think. At this point, you are probably saying to yourself, *"yeah, this person doesn't know me or what I've been through."* My response to that is that I do not have to know what you have been through to know that you are enough. Do you want to know how I know that? I know that because it is a fact.

Chapter 11: Moving On

Sometimes we tend to try to suppress certain feelings and ideas because we fear something or someone. This someone could be ourselves in some cases. I was suppressing the need to add this chapter in this book because it is a sensitive topic. I was not going to touch on this subject, but the more I thought about it, the more I realized how important it was.

There are many who are unable to move on because of the trauma that comes with being subjected to abuse. That trauma keeps them from getting out and rediscovering their previous self and life. Something essential to recognize is that abuse is not just physical, as many people think. It can also be psychological, verbal, or sexual. Whatever the form of abuse, there is no justification for it neither will there ever be.

Recognizing Your Position

Discussing abuse is a very difficult subject, and there are many who refuse to talk about it. The more silent and quiet the person being abused remains, the more powerless they become from rising up and out of their situation in the future. I refuse to stay silent on the subject and keeping my opinions only to myself.

If you are a victim of abuse, get help and become a voice for others who suffer, especially if you have overcome abuse. Many have suffered because of the general fear of talking about something that is as sensitive as abuse, but it's there. It exists and wreaks havoc on the lives of many men and women, who have no other choice but to keep quiet.

Most importantly, I want to enlighten you on the fact that you have the same rights as your perpetrator. It's not like that any specific person was given complete authority over you through a revelation one night. You are not a manually controlled machine or an inanimate object on the shelf. You are a sophisticated human being with a unique and specific personality, aspirations, desires, and needs.

If you are in an undesirable or abusive situation where you feel your life is in danger or you feel you're tired and want a way out, you always have the option to get the help you need. Some might say that they're dependent on their perpetrator and they cannot do anything.

The Cycle of Abuse

You need to understand how bad the situation is first. It's not just you who is suffering at the hands of the harmful person; it's also others, such as children, partners, and employees. So letting the abuse continue is like contributing to further abuse. A saddening fact is that many new perpetrators are born because of abuse. Some people indeed vow to give their kids or partner, for example, the life that they never were able to get.

However, the sad reality is that some become abusers themselves because of the abuse they went through. It's called the cycle of abuse; when victims turn into perpetrators. It is said that abuse usually has a more lasting and negative effect on kids than adults, which is why those who were abused in their early years are much more likely to grow up and abuse than someone who was abused after turning into an adult.

Therefore, if this abuser is not set straight, they are ruining the lives of many and creating more abusive people like themselves. It's an endless cycle. As a victim, you have the ability to reduce the number of people who are harmed. You can do it in two ways.

One is by exposing them and reporting them, so people stay away from them, and that certain person is punished for their destructive behavior. The other is by not letting any of that negativity you experienced during that time turn you negative. That means that you avoid being toxic or violent toward those you interact with, just like your perpetrator did to you.

Advise

You have a considerable amount of control over your life, even when you have someone controlling you. You just need to recognize that you are a living person and not a toy for your abuser to play with. No one deserves to live a life of abuse, but unfortunately, many do. No one should be able to make you feel worthless, insignificant, or a nobody because none of that is true.

You can get out of your situation, but it will take some time, planning, and strategizing on your part. There are people out there who are willing and waiting to help you. I promise they are there; you just need to know where to look. Sometimes you might fight alone in the world, but such is not the case; good people are always there, ready to help.

I'm sorry that life can be really tough sometimes, but just know that you will reach out if you're going through something. This time will pass; you'll make it. Try to surround yourself with people who care for you and love you. This is when you'll start to feel happy, and that is what will heal you.

I understand that it is difficult to move on after you've been abused for years, but honestly, if you do not change afterward, it doesn't get any better. Even after those hard times, you might feel gloomy, depressed, and lonely. You might feel like there is a void inside you that person has created, which is now sucking your soul. This all is valid and understandable but what you need to realize is that you have to bring change into your life in order to heal.

Bring color, creativity, friends, family, studies, art, sports, and entertainment into your life. Try to preoccupy yourself with something you love, and you'll automatically see yourself start to heal. Learn from your extreme experience. However, never let that experience dictate your future. Many people are stuck in a box of negativity after their undesirable situation and fail ever to come out.

Make sure you move on and, more importantly, move up in your life. You might make mistakes along the way, but instead of getting irritated, you learn and grow. We all say and do things that we are not supposed to and do not do or say things that we should. There are moments when you are not proud of yourself, but there is always room for change.

Stop being a perpetrator to yourself. When you stumble, and you think it's too late, pick yourself back up and begin again because there is no such thing as too late. Life is too short for things to be too late!

When we stay in these abusive, toxic, and destructive relationships, we begin to de-self. That means that we start to change according to the needs, preferences, and opinions of the abuser. We try to remain consistent with that perpetrator-gaze. This also means that you would start to lose focus on yourself, and so you'll start to become someone who has no self-worth, self-love, or gratefulness.

Something like this is tremendously harmful. Keep in mind that this can happen to men or women. It can occur in a heterosexual or a homosexual relationship. It can happen from the start or can suddenly surface many years into the relationship. Additionally, note that abusive relationships are not only expressed between a couple. It can also occur within family members, relatives, colleagues, subordinates, and many other groups. By no means am I defining abuse in one dimension! It can be anywhere and everywhere. Regardless of which type of context this abuse is carried out in and whatever type of abuse it is, it is not normal or okay.

If you have done something wrong to someone, you should apologize and try to make up for it. You deserve the best. You deserve better. When you love yourself, this knowledge becomes very apparent.

Chapter 12: All Filled Up

The soul is like a vessel filled with aura and energies that fuel human life. To have a sense of direction and create an objective to live our life – we need inspiration, morals, and conduct. We seek ideologies and guidance to tackle our everyday situations and even our lifelong conundrums. Hence we fill our souls with what we believe will help us survive or thrive. However, sometimes this filling up is confused by an attempt to fill the void originated by loneliness, regret, or anything negative. This void is dangerous because instead of healing your way through it, many people try to fill it with shallow pleasures and distractions.

Others who may really want to heal fill themselves up every day with an enormous dose of encouragement. They allow themselves to seek inspiration, but it somehow ends up overwhelming them. Because the more we move toward the path of improvement, the more hurdles we face in leaving behind our unhealthy habits and patterns. The road to wellness is definitely not easy. The penetration within the heart, mind, and soul releases the frustration of doubt and fear. At times like this, there is a delicate balance to increase the desired level of adaption of change. It can help you sustain and discipline your spirit to stay inclined toward good things.

For instance, I fill myself up with a biblical verse every day while fasting and praying. I anticipate a spiritual breakthrough, and I will not abandon those things that edify me. Whenever we practice doing this, anticipate pushback from unwelcomed energy.

When you begin to enter another spiritual realm, there are powers, principalities, and rulers of darkness that will try to hinder your permissive right Under God (Ephesians 6:12).

When I wrestle against these powers, I have an advocate who represents me when I fall or fail. We have a right to rebuke and bind those things that hinder us from our preordained Destiny (2 Corinthians 10:3-5).

Surrounding ourselves with positivity works, but we have to reciprocate with it in order to make the most of it. The modern world is an ocean of information overflowed; one button and we have all the positive quotes of the world on our phone but is it enough? It is certainly not. Positivity will not change you unless you put it in motion with your energy. Hearing positive words and being encouraged is good, but we need to also act on what we hear. When you have been drained in negativity for the long term, it takes extra effort to implement the right things in your life. However, unless we exert the energy to indulge ourselves in positive actions, activities, and thinking, we will not be able to have the transformation we need.

The Courage To Be Better

It often seems effortless and pleasant from afar, but true self-care can be difficult. It takes courage to push yourself to do the things you need to do and leave the comfort of sadness that keeps you free from the responsibility to make your life better.

One of the things that stop us from taking revolutionary initiatives is the negativity we consume unconsciously. The vessel of our soul is hypersensitive and adaptable. That is why we must become conscious about what we consume with all five senses. For example, if all you hear is self-defeating dialogue all day, it will taint your reflection and perspective about the world. Melancholy will surround you like a thick cloud.

The content we consume is another significant element that decides our energy and spiritual wellness. If one watches self-defeating content all day, their conscious and unconscious mind dwells on a similar frequency spreading the poison of hopelessness and ambiguity. If you are continually consuming negative or pessimistic content, you cannot be filled up with the right things. If you are frequently around people who offer no hope and lackadaisical, you are bound to exhibit the same behavior.

Choose To Be Undaunted By Your Trials

When we are going through hard times, it often gets hard to be honest with ourselves. To soothe our hurt selves, we often spiral in self-pity and indulge in content that validates our negative feelings. This, however, affects us badly because it only enhances the negative sentiments we are already suffering from without offering any solution or strength to solve the problem. At times, it gets extremely hard to override these emotions and rise above the fog of sadness and despair, but we must remind ourselves that only if we push through it will we make it to the other side, where positivity and good things await us.

The best possible action in such situations is to be honest and self-aware. It is so important to check our emotions and reevaluate feelings and situations. Take stock of what is really going on and investigate your emotions, whether it is someone else causing your dismay or things are just out of control for whatever reason. Just know there is light at the end of the tunnel, and this too shall pass.

It is like encountering a big giant when we ourselves feel so small. Problems and pain can leave us paralyzed with their severity. These are the times when you need to keep the logical eye open with all the calmness you have. When our senses are heightened with emotions, our mind's automated response is an exaggeration of everything that comes in front of us. Even if the problem is bigger than your resources, losing hope and giving up cannot lead you to a good place. Choose to be undaunted by the trials and tribulations that come your way.

In the darkest moment of our life, when pain pierces through our soul, and it becomes difficult to breathe, we feel like a spiritual death has embraced us, and we can never be alive again. I know the feeling because I have been through it.

There have been times when I wanted to give up and give in because the pain that penetrated my being seemed too great. I just wanted the pain to stop and leave every part of my being. How can I stop it from permeating every inch of my heart, soul, and mind? It was a struggle that I can never forget, but in the end, I am glad that I made it through it.

The secret is never to give in the face of an adversary no matter how cruel it gets – know that time and constant hard work is bound to pay off at one point. Every inspiration story, every person who has been through the immense pain and depression in their lives and has defeated it will tell you the same. Words, situations, and people can be different, but the message is the same; no matter how brutal it gets – never give up, but forge ahead. Knowing that pain is necessary for our growth helps us to fuel our determination and resilience.

An athlete knows what it takes to reach the pinnacle of success. They must discipline their mind, body, and soul and practice every day despite the ache in every muscle. A farmer knows he has to plow the soil till the land spurs with a prosperous harvest. A presenter who has to give a speech to a massive crowd knows that he has to fight the shiver under his skin and the fear of failing. They all know too well what it takes to make a difference, and hard work will get the job done. Therefore when life knocks you out, and you fall hard, *brace yourself for the pain and get back on your feet. Choose to be undaunted by the trials and tribulations that come your way. The moment you decide to face the situation and lock your horn with it – it will become easier. Once you take the first step toward the solution, you feel confident spurring in your nerve toward healing. A small ray of hope will lighten up your soul, and in its light, you will gradually move forward. This is a pattern of life. Believe it or not, everyone goes through a situation or more that changes their reality and causes them intense pain but what we do with that pain is upon us.

We all have been given our own test in life. The test can be easy or challenging and oftentimes unfair. The dice rolls, and we all get a share of life's most horrific nightmares; we all get our share of sadness. For me, the most significant test is the test of time because it waits for no man. It makes us bid goodbye to our loved ones, leaving us with nothing but the fondest of memories. It also seems as if we never have enough time to right our wrongs or achieve our fondest desires.

Sometimes time is not on our side, and we are left wondering how we could turn back the hands of time. In almost every phase of our life, we wish to turn back and correct things; sometimes, we want it to stay and freeze it forever, but the haunted void left by time can be tricky to deal with. Nostalgia, when it becomes overpowering, can hinder our progress toward the future. Don't let the sands of time hold you back, even if the pathway seems daunting.

Chapter 13: Stressed

There are all kinds of sadness lurking among humans. At times, the sadness originates from a wound, or prejudice, a deception that breaks our trust and our souls. Other times the origin of sorrow is unknown – it seeps into our bones quietly, taking over our life. The reason can be any, but all sadness extracts from one element: lack of hope. Hope is the ultimate food of the soul. It keeps the spirit alive – it gives us the reason to live, to look forward to the days ahead of us, but when there is no hope, we lose the meaning of life, and everything seems useless. The roots of our everyday stress grow into the soil of a hope crisis.

Moreover, when we try to improve the situation or look for help, and nothing turns our way – we are even more stressed. The blistering agony of unanswered prayers can leave us in a hopeless state. The misery of hopelessness and despair can cause destruction that goes deeper than the surface level depression.

The mind-numbing paranoia and anxiety capture our every second. Hence, once we leave our depression unchecked and let it settle into our souls, stress begins to take on a completely new meaning, and the body aches with despair. Our thoughts and feelings affect our health immensely. Hence, it is crucial not to let the stressors of life wear you down. I know that our circumstances can sometimes overwhelm us. I have been through immense pain, where I felt like I will not be able to breathe. That is why I understand how stress decreases our mental ability to cope with the situation. Nevertheless, do not let stress overtake your physical, psychological, and emotional well-being.

This is the reason that our anxiety disturbs our eating and sleeping orders. As we continuously try to attain peace and keep melancholy at bay, we exert all our energy endlessly, and hence our body starts showing the symptoms of extreme exhaustion. If we do not rise above the ocean of grief to breathe, our existence becomes stagnant, and our health begins to decay.

We experience physical health problems, and our immune system breaks down, making us vulnerable to unwanted illnesses. The better we can conquer our negative emotions, the better off we will be to ward off unhealthy illnesses waiting to dominate our bodies. That is why it is essential to have a bigger perspective on life. Instead of dwelling in the painful past or worrying about the distant future, learn to live in the present. Motivate yourself beyond the daily stressors of life so that you can be at your optimal best.

Coping Mechanisms

We are known to react to stress in a fight or flight response because we naturally become defensive when we feel threatened. Stressors in this hyperactive world are almost unavoidable, but to cope with these waves of worry, one can undoubtedly develop healthy habits and thought patterns. We often state coping mechanisms as negative, but they can also be positive and help you sustain through difficult times. If you have coping mechanisms that can help you feel less stressed, you are one step ahead of the game. However, harmful coping mechanisms such as denial or fear of attachment, etc., derange your body and soul's energy. Those who are consistently negative or have inadequate coping mechanisms are more likely to experience internal physical problems.

Hence, we must keep in check our routine and thought patterns positively. Unconscious but constant negative thinking puts us in a bad mood and exposes us to the risk of laziness and denial. We then start neglecting a healthy lifestyle of optimism, positive thinking, and hope are a few of the major components needed to feel better about yourself. Once a person has created a non-threatening lifestyle for themselves, they can move forward and establish a reduction of stress in their lives for the future. Hope is the belief we grab hold of to achieve our highest goals. Optimism is an expected outcome that these Things will occur in the face of setbacks, obstacles, or negative circumstances. Hope and optimism can be seen as the same because they can both provide a healing quality to what ails the human body and mind.

When I was confined in my depression, I trained my mind to stay on the upbeat track of thoughts. I had to practice changing my thought process with healthy ideas when negative thinking tries to take over. Changing the distortions of negative thinking that exaggerate, overgeneralize, and keep you feeling downtrodden is never conducive to one's thought process. However, this was not an easy journey. When you are deciphering through the pathways of wellness, they are not always clear. One goes through many stages of doubt, fear, and sadness before they are sure of their decisions and actions.

Guilt and Regret In Recovery

I used to feel ashamed of trying to achieve my desired goals. I was deeply apologetic. I felt I was selfish for wanting to have more and be more in life. I later in my life realized that guilt and shame could interfere with one trying to establish their goals. We are often too afraid to make a bad impression of others and be the target of people's judgment. The fear of our weaknesses being revealed to people can destroy our self-confidence to follow our dreams. It is both; a private and public humiliation that can make one feel abandoned and isolated from others.

That is why it is important to have good company around you. Having good social support systems such as family, friends, community, church, support groups can help strengthen your resolve. The foundation of one's personality development starts with parenting. If the parent can bond with their child to develop a secure feeling, then the child can become more confident. People with stronger support systems are known to be happier and healthier. They have a secure attachment style and reflect confidence and independence. They have the ability to overcome their obstacles sooner because they have an emotional support system in place.

On the other hand, children who have seen physical or emotional abuse in childhood are scarred with cruel memories that later affect their belief system. Identity crisis is much bigger for adults who have a troubled childhood. However, healing is always possible if you choose it over victimization and excuses not to be better.

People who have recovered from such a situation have a strong will to be better than what they have seen and faced. When unfavorable circumstances arise, they have an outlet that will help them recover and recuperate. We can all learn to create happiness by developing healthy relationships and caring for others, even looking at our history, mainly ancestral, to develop an idea of how our ties to kinship can make us stronger. Surround yourself around those who value your unique qualities and opinions. Take healthy risks and believe that something good will happen. Taking risks can lead to lucrative outcomes and will never lead to regret.

Locus Of Control[1]

I firmly believe in the mental capabilities of an individual to make improvements in their personality and life. One of

---

[1] J.B. Rotter. (1966). Generalized expectancies for internal versus external control of reinforcement. Psychological Monographs, 80, (one, Whole No. 609).

the theories that support this concept is the Locus of Control. Locus of Control is defined as a concept in which one believes they control their destiny and what influences their life. Your internal locus of control should dominate your external locus of control when pursuing your ultimate desires. (Rotter J.B, 1966).

However, you can fall somewhere between the two LOC's. If you find that you have more of an external locus of control, you can change self-dialogue. For instance, self-talk statements like; There is no point in setting goals or just no use; life is not fair. Those who use the internal locus of control concept use "I" statements to maximize their future endeavors. They will use statements of determination; I am successful, or I will get the job. The Locus of Control is the design of Psychologist Julian Rotter, who also created a Locus of Control scale. The test helps those who would like to know if they fall under an internal or external belief system. These are just a few coping mechanisms I refer to from varying therapeutic concepts.

Psychology and the concept of mindfulness have evolved so much that today we are better equipped to deal with our mental and spiritual crises. That is why even though I am not a licensed therapist; I feel the information is useful in guiding one to understand them better. Yet, the Locus of Control is only one of the many beneficial concepts that can help the mind open the door of consciousness and invite positivity in life. Remember that the mind is a powerful place to imagine, fantasize; more importantly, it can make all things possible only if you place your faith in it.

Chapter 14: Spiritual Journey

Sometimes we have to go before the throne of grace and mercy. We need someone to intercede on our behalf. Trying to do all these things on your own will never work. When you decide to press forward, when you get sick and tired of being sick and tired, then you're ready.

From my personal journal, I wrote these words during a very dark time in my life.

First Entry On October 1st Reads:

Well Lord, here we are again! Today is a beautiful bright sunny day in October, but I still feel under the weather. This depression has been so hard for me. Will you ever deliver me from it, Lord? I know that if you are willing, I can be healed. For some reason, you do not choose to do so. I am not okay with that, but I am learning to be patient in long-suffering, gentle to those around me.

This has truly been a humbling experience. I feel so alone even though I have the support of my family and friends around me. Lord, give me the strength to deal with these weaknesses in my life. Lord, give me something to ease my mind until I can overcome this difficult time.

2nd Entry On October 5 Reads

Lord, thank you for this day and every day you have given me. The choices that are made every day may not always be what I want, but I am glad that you are in every decision I make. When things come against your children, you are there to shelter us and encompass us all around.

I know that you order my steps and that *"no weapon formed against me shall prosper, and every tongue which rises against me in judgment You shall condemn. This is the heritage of the servants of The Lord."* Isaiah 54:17.

I also know that to be anxious about anything is not good. For your word says, *"Be anxious for nothing, but in everything by prayer and supplication, with thanksgiving, let your requests be made known to God; and the peace of God, which surpasses all understanding, will guard your hearts and minds through Jesus Christ."* Philippians 4:6-7.

We live in a world that tries to dictate how we should live, the lifestyle choices that we should make for ourselves, but Lord, you have given us the privilege to be free from worldly demands. We can store our treasures in heaven, where neither moth nor rust can eat, nor do thieves steal. I know my mind is being renewed day by day. For I choose not to be conformed to this world but transformed by the renewing of my mind – this too shall pass.

These passages in my journal were written many, many years ago, and today I have seen the Lord's loving hands heal and guide me through it all. I thought it was significant to share because not many people are vulnerable enough to share their moments of weakness. They always want to look strong and in control when, in reality, they are suffering inside. Sharing these passages with you makes me realize that I am an overcomer in my journey and that my past, present, and momentary weaknesses DO NOT define me. They do not define you either. Get out there!

For instance, Psalmist David from the bible wasn't perfect and made many mistakes, but that didn't stop him from pursuing his spiritual journey. If you are on a spiritual journey, just know that waiting on the Lord can be difficult as we anticipate answered prayer. Moses became angry in his journey and, as a result, didn't enter the promised land.

There have been many times, as I mentioned before, that I let my anger get the best of me with the uneasiness of life's circumstances. However, praying for God's guidance, direction, and forgiveness has sustained me. The opposition, hurdles, and roadblocks have taught me to pray even more fervently. The curveballs will come like most and these moments are only there to help us complete our mission.

Feel confident and hopeful in your journey right now. It is okay to question even if God might be blocking things for a greater purpose. There could be many giants in your life, and you might feel that you don't have the fortitude to stand against them, but you can have faith as a small mustard seed to defeat them...yes, yes, yes, you will defeat them!

My struggle with perfectionism was killing me inwardly and outwardly, but I came to the realization that the only perfect person in my life was Jesus himself. Allow God to do his work in your life no matter how it looks to others. Look at the disciples who followed Jesus, and you will see that they were broken, legalistic, and self-serving before coming to know him.

God wants to realign our hearts and make a change. There are too often times when the enemy tries to steal our joy and tries to distract us away from God's purpose. As he equips us to do whatever the call is for our lives, the enemy puts doubt and fear in our minds and hearts. Realize that there could be a period of pause or uncertainty as he draws you closer to your calling in life. To get your attention, he puts things around you that are constant reminders that he is in control.

We have to realize that it's not my will that will be done but God, Yours. When we struggle with denial, addiction, lying, anger, frustration, grief, depression, suicidal thoughts, we need to trust in God even more. Be honest with yourself and with him and cry out to him and let him know how you feel. I remember dropping to my knees one day and crying out to him as loud as I could. A change immediately took place. An unexpected change that I had no idea would occur so expediently. There are times it will not always happen that way and could take even longer, but it is better to cry out to him anyway in expectation for needed healing. Did you hear me? You have to call out and say, "Jesus, I don't know what I did in life to deserve this life, I don't know where to start to begin my healing, and I need a change, help me, Lord now!

Humbly go before him and seek his face, and don't allow for any distractions. Jesus is waiting to hear from you, and he wants you to need him. Accept what is going on in your life and actually embrace it with open arms. When the equilibrium of life becomes unbalanced, we have to assess that moment more thoroughly.

You can get through the shame and guilt of life if that's what you're experiencing. No one has a right to look at you sideways and point fingers at you because of your past or present situation. The Lord says that *"None is righteous, no, not one, no one understands; no one seeks for God. All have turned aside; together, they have become worthless; no one does good, not even one."* Romans 3:11-12.

"All of us have become like one who is unclean, and all our righteous acts are like filthy rags; we all shrivel up like a leaf, and like the wind, our sins sweep us away." Isaiah 64:6.

If you, at any point in time, feel like you can't do whatever it is that you desire to do, then make a list of all those things. Even if the list doesn't help motivate you, then list the reason why you're unable to. This is a strategy that is bound to help you achieve your wildest dreams.

Your list can look something like the example that follows:

1- Start my new business

2- Finish my documentary

3- Develop meaningful relationships

4- Read five books throughout the year

5- Learn digital arts

Then, you can list down some of the reasons why you are unable to achieve such objectives.

1- I can't stop feeling intimidated by others, which is why I am unable to gather the courage to ...

2- I can't forgive others and that ...

Whatever it is in your life that has led you to believe in the "I Can't" ideology, remove it from your life.

The way you can do that is by following the format below.

I Can_____

But I don't because _____

I will no longer say "I Can't" because _____

The significance of this way to go about it is that it gives you a written answer to what is bothering you the most and how you can resolve your problem.

If you are finding that there are more things you can't do than you can do, examine why. You have to be totally honest with yourself and set realistic expectations. When you say you can't, are you convincing yourself that this is a factual statement, or is it just that you are demotivated?

We can turn our back on God, but he will never leave us or forsake us. He sees all that we are and all that we can become; he can see our potential. So often, we walk by sight and can only see what is in front of us. We never take the time to notice and appreciate what we don't see. There could be people in your life who see you but don't really see you. They don't see your ability to rise above your circumstances and your ability to fan the flames of failure, regret, and disappointment. You are a resilient human being and unstoppable in all your ways.

Who told you that you weren't enough or that you didn't have what it takes to make a difference? Stop listening to those people and know that God has got you! He knows the number of hairs on your head and how many tears you have cried. He collects your tears and bottles them up, feeling every ache and the pain you endure.

The hard truth doesn't look good at times and can be an unending stench of reality. However, without the truth, we don't get a chance to see the beauty that is beneath. Our hearts and minds' inner workings are ever-changing when we embrace the reality of God's love for us—breaking news Flash! You are loved even at your worse, even when you're unkind because you felt like venting your anger on someone else.

If you can apologize to that person and make amends for hurting them, you are winning. Sometimes we say things to a person and never have the opportunity to apologize or hold them one last time. We feel they will be with us forever and that we can say sorry tomorrow or the next day. Tomorrow is not a guarantee, and every day we hold a grudge against someone is a day we lose. The loss is ever-changing, and there is no turning back from that moment.

Chapter 15: The Beginning

You have come to the end of the book now. You might be feeling a certain emotion, or maybe it's a sea of emotions. Some of you might be glad that this book is finally over, and now you can simply put it back on the bookshelf, while some of you might be reading these last couple hundreds of words with a heavy heart.

I want to inform you that just the fact that you not only bought this book but also read it to the end shows something. It shows that you are a determined individual who is willing to change and improve. This willingness to improve and put oneself out there is a trait that can get you quite far in life.

Now that we are almost at the end, it is important for you to know what to do next; you need to have direction. The next step is literally to change. You've read about all the dimensions change expands into, so there's a lot that you can choose from. You've read it all, and now it's time to implement everything.

I would highly recommend that you keep this book in an easily accessible place like your desk so every time you see it lying around, you are instantly reminded about change. Another recommendation is to keep referring back to this book to keep the ideas and tips fresh in your mind.

Now comes the big question. Where do you begin? Where should one start his/her revolutionary journey? If you're unsure where to begin, one simple solution is just starting right where you are. If the thing that is currently bothering you is work, then begin with work. If the biggest problem you're currently facing is being unable to connect to people, work on that first. Start with what is influencing you the most right now.

Additionally, also try to keep a journal of your visions and objectives. Write any and everything that comes to mind, no matter how unnecessary and childish you feel it is. Acknowledge and empower yourself each day by writing something that is personal to you on your calendar that you can hang on your wall or keep on your desk.

I have a calendar myself. It's one that has small extracts from the book of Psalms. So, for the entire week or each day, I write "Never Stop Believing" or any other motivational sentence. It helps; it really does. Believe in yourself even if those around you don't believe in you. Always know one thing. People see you the way you see yourself.

So, if you care for yourself and love yourself, people will automatically be attracted to your personality. I am aware that it might sound cliché, but self-care is very important. You can write daily, weekly, or monthly aspirations of encouragement as a way to help you overcome self-hatred and the lack of confidence.

Most of all, don't give up on yourself. You are enough as you are no matter what others say. We all are humans, so it's impossible to be flawless. Just keep on working on yourself and developing yourself, and eventually, you'll get to the place you always wanted to be. That's a guarantee given you always keep an open mind and adhere to perseverance.

If you're religious, stay grateful for everything that you have to whomever you worship. Even if you aren't religious, every one of us is blessed to great extents. I believe that being thankful to God only results in him granting more and more. He loves all of us, and he tests us by giving us more than others or less than others.

Remember that it's okay to laugh at yourself from time to time and not to take life too seriously as well. Develop a jolly personality. Talk to people about things you love and laugh with them. You must have heard the common phrase: laughter is the best medicine. Laugh at yourself, and laugh at yourself with others. Keep things light-hearted. The world is a very dark place, and your laughter will make it a better place for you and many others.

Believe me; I've had to laugh at myself a number of times to get here. The more you laugh, the softer your heart becomes, and the more positive you see in even the most negative of things.

"A cheerful heart is a good medicine, but a broken spirit saps a person's strength." Proverbs 17:2

Just remember to laugh when you can because it is a well-known fact that laughter releases endorphins in the brain, giving you a euphoric feeling. Laughter also relieves stress and improves your outlook. We all wrestle with the uncertainties of life and wonder how we can live our lives without feeling worthless. We wonder if our lives really made a difference or if we have just been living to survive instead of living to live.

I hope this book has answered some of your questions. If you have ever doubted your purpose in life, I hope this book has helped you reduce that. I hope this book has turned that tiny whisper within you into a roar. I hope that all the sleepless nights that you spent overthinking are transformed into peaceful nights where you dream of the very bliss that will be your future.

Everyone gets some sort of an opportunity at some point in their lives, but not everyone gets a second chance. Some are restricted to only one chance, one opportunity. So when you get your opportunity, grab it because you never know if you will get a second one because always know that life is uncertain.

You might be able to make a difference in someone's life as well as your own. Take it; you will not regret it. You'll regret it more if you don't take advantage of your opportunities. Always know that if you work on something, it will always have a positive effect somehow. Even if, for example, you work super hard for a test and yet still somehow fail, you actually learned a lot still.

Usually, any sort of self-development will come to fruition, and you must believe in that. Even if it seems it was all for nothing at first, just tread on, and you will start to see the fruits of your labor manifest as you desired. It's all about perseverance and change, as I have said many times before.

As a parting piece of advice that you'll overtime realize is always be your true and unapologetic self. You are perfect as you are, so live like that. Voice your opinions where needed and try not to fear judgment. You don't need to force your opinions on others.

Be you, whether the context is home, college, workplace, friends, relatives, etc. Just always be yourself. You don't need to change yourself because someone said you wouldn't fit it like this. You are who you are, and the true people will love you for who you are.

Therefore, I am truthfully and unapologetically

T. Raheyyu Hope and **YES, YOU CAN!**

Notes

Notes

Notes

Notes

Notes

Notes

T. RAHEYYU HOPE

Made in the USA
Middletown, DE
10 September 2021